Easy Microsoft
Outlook® 97

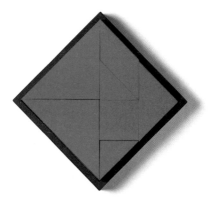

Jennifer Fulton

Easy Microsoft Outlook 97

Library of Congress Catalog Card Number: 96-72204

International Standard Book Number: 0-7897-1141-9

99 98   8 7 6 5 4 3 2

Interpretation of the printing code: The rightmost double-digit number is the year of the book's first printing; the rightmost single-digit number is the number of the book's printing. For example, a printing code of 97-1 shows that this copy of the book was printed during the first printing of the book in 1997.

Screen reproductions in this book were created by means of the program Collage Complete from Inner Media, Inc., Hollis, NH.

This book was produced digitally by Macmillan Computer Publishing and manufactured using computer-to-plate technology (a film-less process) by GAC/Shepard Poorman, Indianapolis, Indiana.

Printed in the United States of America.

Dedication

To my husband Scott, who completes me.

Credits

Publisher
Roland Elgey

Publishing Manager
Lynn E. Zingraf

Editorial Services Director
Elizabeth Keaffaber

Managing Editor
Michael Cunningham

Director of Marketing
Lynn E. Zingraf

Acquisitions Editor
Martha O'Sullivan

Technical Specialist
Nadeem Muhammed

Product Development Specialists
Melanie Palaisa
Henly Wolin

Technical Editor
Keith Whitemore

Production Editor
Katie Purdum

Book Designers
Barbara Kordesh
Ruth Harvey

Cover Designers
Dan Armstrong
Kim Scott

Production Team
Erin M. Danielson, DiMonique Ford,
Trey Frank, Julie Geeting, Tim Neville,
Kaylene Riemen, Julie Searls, Sossity
Smith

Indexer
Tim Tate

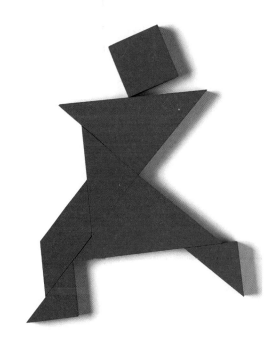

Composed in *Syntax* and *New Century Schoolbook* by Que Corporation

We'd Like to Hear from You!

As part of our continuing effort to produce books of the highest possible quality, Que would like to hear your comments. To stay competitive, we really want you, as a computer book reader and user, to let us know what you like or dislike most about this book or other Que products.

You can mail comments, ideas, or suggestions for improving future editions to the address below, or send us a fax at (317) 581-4663. For the online inclined, Macmillan Computer Publishing has a forum on CompuServe (type **GO QUEBOOKS** at any prompt) through which our staff and authors are available for questions and comments. The address of our Internet site is **http://www.quecorp.com** (World Wide Web).

In addition to exploring our forum, please feel free to contact me personally to discuss your opinions of this book: I'm **73353,2061** on CompuServe, and I'm **mpalaisa@que.mcp.com** on the Internet.

Although we cannot provide general technical support, we're happy to help you resolve problems you encounter related to our books, disks, or other products. If you need such assistance, please contact our Tech Support department at 800-545-5914 ext. 3833.

To order other Que or Macmillan Computer Publishing books or products, please call our Customer Service department at 800-835-3202 ext. 666.

Thanks in advance—your comments will help us to continue publishing the best books available on computer topics in today's market.

Melanie Palaisa
Product Development Specialist
Que Corporation
201 W. 103rd Street
Indianapolis, Indiana 46290
USA

About the Author

After years of working with computers, Jennifer brings what's left of her sense of humor along with her vast experiences to each of her books, including *Easy Outlook, Netscape Navigator 6-in-1, The Big Basics Book of the Internet, The Big Basics Book of Windows 95,* and *The Big Basics Book of Office 97.* Jennifer and her husband Scott (another computer book author) live in a home filled with many books, some of which they did not write.

Acknowledgments

I'd like to thank everyone who worked on this book, especially Melanie Palaisa, Henly Wolan, and Katie Purdum. I know that sometimes it seemed as if none of us would ever see daylight again, but the sun's sure shining now! Thanks for all the hard work.

Trademarks

All terms mentioned in this book that are known to be trademarks or service marks have been appropriately capitalized. Que Corporation cannot attest to the accuracy of this information. Use of a term in this book should not be regarded as affecting the validity of any trademark or service mark.

Contents

Contents

Part X: Reference   231

Index   246

Introduction

What You Can Do with Outlook

Instead of using a paper-based day planner to organize your busy life, why not use Microsoft Outlook instead? It contains many programs which perform the same functions as the sections in a typical day planner: address book, calendar, task list, and a place for your notes. But because Microsoft Outlook is a computer program, you can do a lot more with it than you could with an ordinary day planner. The following list helps to illustrate this point.

With the Inbox section of Outlook, you can:

- Send and receive e-mail messages over any messaging system to which you have access, such as a company network, an intranet, or the Internet.

- If you use CompuServe, America Online, Microsoft Network (MSN), Prodigy, and so on, you can send and receive messages from these services as well.

- Send and receive faxes (provided you have a fax modem).

- Add voting buttons to a message to enable the recipients to "vote" on a particular option or plan.

- Use Microsoft Word as your e-mail editor, and get the full benefit of its tools, such as automatic spelling correction, bulleted lists, numbered lists, and tables.

With the Calendar section of Outlook, you can:

- Schedule your appointments, and move them easily.

- Schedule meetings with coworkers and book the room, and other resources you'll need.

- Schedule other special events, such as your anniversary.

- Schedule holidays and other recurring events.

With the Contacts section of Outlook, you can:

- Keep track of the important people in your life, such as sales contacts, coworkers, family, friends, and so on.

- Record important home and business address, phone numbers, fax numbers, e-mail addresses, and other pertinent information for each contact.

- Call any contact with the click of a button.

With the Tasks section of Outlook, you can:

- Prioritize tasks, and track your progress.

- Set up reminders so you don't forget to do important tasks.

- Assign tasks to other people, and keep track of their progress.

- Produce status reports for the tasks to which you've been assigned.

With the Journal section of Outlook, you can:

- Organize your thoughts.

- Automatically track your activities.

- Record the documents you've worked on recently, and open them again with a click.

With the Notes section of Outlook, you can:

- Jot down quick notes, and not lose track of them!

- Store small bits of information, such as directions to a client's office, or travel data.

All of the parts in Outlook work together. For example, you can easily create a journal entry or an e-mail message for anyone in your contact list. Outlook also works with your other Office 97 programs, such as Word, Excel, PowerPoint, and Access. You can use the names in your contact list to create a mass mailing using Microsoft Word.

Outlook provides quick access to your files through its My Computer icon, and My Documents and Favorites folders. You'll find that it's easy to create new Office documents from within Outlook.

Although Outlook is powerful, you'll find it easy to use. The Outlook bar provides quick access to the different sections, and the toolbars keep the tools you need close at hand. In addition, Outlook is customizable, so you can change it to suit your specific needs.

Task Sections

The Task sections include the steps for accomplishing a certain task (such as creating a new e-mail message or a new contact). The numbered steps walk you through a specific example so that you can learn the task by actually doing it.

Big Screen

At the beginning of each task is a large picture of your PC screen showing the results of the task or some other key element from the task (such as a menu or dialog box).

"Why would I do this?"

Each task includes a brief explanation of why you would benefit from knowing how to accomplish the task.

TASK

6

Changing Views and How Information Is Sorted

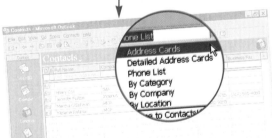

"Why would I do this?"

Each of Outlook's programs displays its information in a particular way. You can change the way in which information is displayed by changing the view. For example, the items in the Contacts list are typically displayed as a phone list, with each person and his phone numbers shown on a separate line. You can change to a different view if you want. For example, you could select a view that displays each person's phone numbers and e-mail addresses in a card format.

You can also change the order in which information is displayed. Items in each Outlook section are always sorted in a particular order. For example, the items in the Inbox are sorted by the date they are received, from the most recent message to the oldest. You can reverse the order of how information is displayed or you can change the column by which the information is sorted. For example, you can have items sorted by the received date or by the name of the person who sent them.

26

Step-by-Step Screens

Each task includes a screen shot for each step of the procedure. The screen shot shows how the computer screen looks at each step in the process.

■▲●■▲●■▲●■▲●■

Task 6: Changing Views and How Information Is Sorted

1 To change to a different view, open the **Current View** list on the Standard toolbar and select the view you want. For example, the Contacts list initially displays each item on a separate line. To display the items in a card format, select **Address Cards** from the Current View list.

Puzzled?

If you select a view you don't like, simply open the **Current View** list, and select a different view.

Puzzled? Notes

The Puzzled? notes tell you how to undo certain procedures or how to get out of unexpected situations.

2 To reverse the order of how items are sorted, click the button marked by the arrow. In the Inbox, click the **Received** button to reverse the sort order.

Missing Link

You can also sort items by their category (such as business or personal), or by their group (such as company or state).

3 To sort by a different column (field), click that column's header (title) instead. For example, click the **From** header, and the items in the Inbox are sorted by the person who sent them. ■

Missing Link

You may be able to display a preview pane at the bottom of the Inbox Window. See Task 10.

Missing Link Notes

Missing Link notes that tell you a little more about the procedure. For example, these notes may define terms, explain other options, refer you to other sections, or provide hints and shortcuts.

27

5

▲●■▲●■▲●■

PART I

Getting Started Quickly

▲ ● ■ ■ ▲ ● ■ ▲ ●

MICROSOFT OUTLOOK IS AN ELECTRONIC DAY PLANNER that enables you to keep track of important information such as appointments, meetings, contact names and phone numbers, e-mail addresses, and the like. If you've installed other Office 97 programs such as Word, Excel, or PowerPoint, you'll find that Outlook works easily with those programs to allow you complete access to your information. For example, if you want to include a sales worksheet created in Excel within an Outlook e-mail message, the process is as easy as drag-and-drop (dragging the file into a message and dropping it).

Outlook contains an e-mail program, a calendar, an address book, a to-do list, journal, and notepad. In addition, Outlook serves as a miniature version of Windows Explorer, providing complete access to your files—whether they're located on your system, or on your company's network. Through Outlook, you can search for a file, open it, make changes, and even insert that file into an Outlook document, such as an e-mail message, a Calendar entry, or your Journal.

As you use each of Outlook's various programs, you'll notice a lot of similarities. Each section uses the same menu bar, with the addition of an extra menu customized for that section. To select a command off a menu, click the menu name (such as File) and then click the command you want (such as Print).

Underneath the menu bar is the Standard toolbar. There are several buttons on this toolbar that appear regardless of where you are in Outlook:

New   Add a new entry. When you click this button in the Inbox, you create a new e-mail message. If you're in Calendar, you create a new appointment.

Back   Move back to a previous entry.

Forward   Move forward to the next entry.

Up One Level   Move up one folder (directory) level.

Folder List   Display the Folder List, which allows you to switch between the various sections in Outlook as you might switch between folders in Explorer.

Print   Print the entries in the current section.

Print Preview   View what will be printed, before it's printed.

Office Assistant   Get help with an Outlook feature.

Additional buttons, applicable to that part, appear at the end of the toolbar as you move from section to section in Outlook. The toolbar that links all of Outlook's various programs together is the Outlook bar, which you'll find located on the left side of the Outlook window. The Outlook bar is divided into sections:

Outlook   Here you'll find icons for each of the Outlook parts.

Mail   Here you'll find icons for the different parts of the messaging system.

Other   Through this part of the Outlook bar, you can access your files.

In this part, you'll be exposed to each of Outlook's various programs: Inbox, Calendar, Contacts, Tasks, Journal, and Notes. In addition, you'll learn how to access documents from within Outlook. You'll also see how to adjust your view within a particular program, get help, and exit Outlook safely.

1

Starting Microsoft Outlook

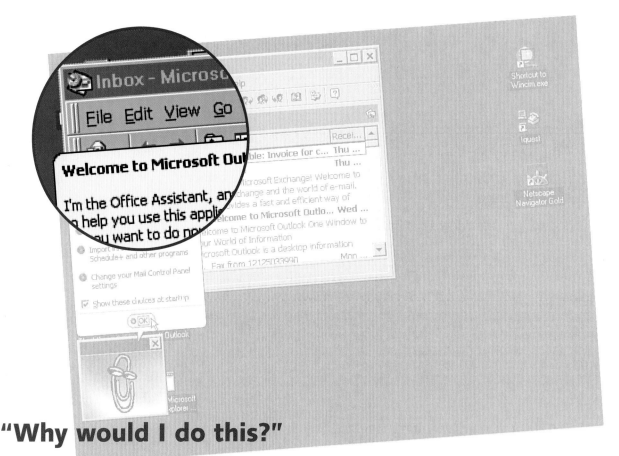

"Why would I do this?"

In order to use the features in Microsoft Outlook, you first have to turn on your computer, and then you start the program. After you start Outlook, you can work within any of its various sections.

How you start the program depends on whether or not you've installed the Office Shortcut Bar. The Shortcut Bar

is not installed if you select the Typical installation option—although you can install it easily enough by simply running the Setup program again. (See the Reference section if you need help.) Follow Steps 1–4 if you did not install the Shortcut Bar; follow Steps 5–6 if you have installed it.

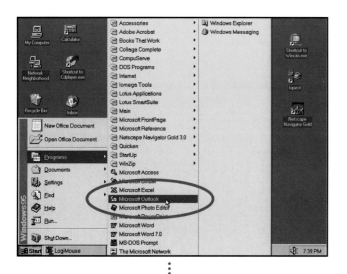

1 Click the **Start** button on the Windows 95 taskbar. The Start menu appears. Typically, Microsoft places its program items on the main Programs menu. Using your mouse, point to **Programs**, and the Programs menu appears. Move the mouse over **Microsoft Outlook** and click.

Puzzled?

If you mistakenly start the wrong program by clicking its name, close that program and perform Step 1 again.

2 When you start Microsoft Outlook for the first time, you're greeted by the Office Assistant. If you don't want to see this list of options, click **Show these choices at startup** to deselect it. To begin Outlook, click **OK** in the Office Assistant.

Missing Link

Learn about Outlook before you start using it by clicking **See key information for upgraders and new users** in the Office Assistant. A dialog box will list new features. When you are finished, click **OK**.

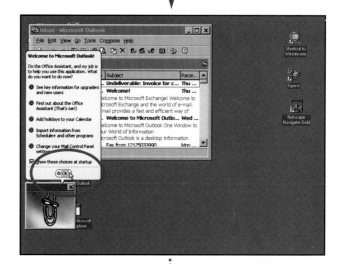

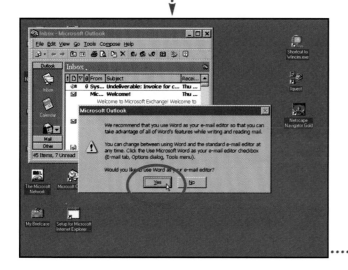

3 The first time you start Outlook, it asks if you'd like to use Word as your e-mail editor. Using Word allows flexibility when creating e-mail messages because you can use all of its features. Click **Yes** or **No**.

Puzzled?

You can turn the Word editor ON or OFF as needed, by opening the **Tools** menu, selecting **Options**, and clicking the **E-Mail** tab. Click the option, **Use Microsoft Word as the e-mail editor**, then click **OK**.

Task 1: Starting Microsoft Outlook

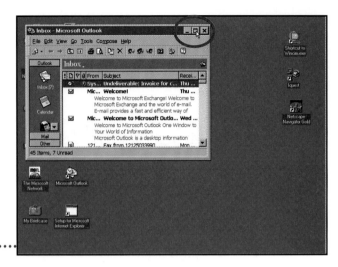

4 When Outlook starts for the first time, it starts in a small window. You might prefer to use Outlook this way in order to view its data while working in another program. If you prefer to maximize that window, click the **Maximize** button (which you'll find in the upper right corner).

5 If the Office Shortcut Bar appears on your desktop, you can use it to open Outlook. Click the **Microsoft Outlook** button. You can start other Office programs from the Shortcut bar by clicking the appropriate button. Move the mouse pointer over a button and leave it there. A label will appear, identifying the button.

> **Puzzled?**
>
> If the Office icons are not displayed, click the icon at the bottom of the Shortcut bar. If the icon does not appear, right-click an open area of the Shortcut bar and select **Office**.

6 If you want to open Outlook to perform a specific task, there are additional buttons on the Office Shortcut Bar which you can use. For example, to create a quick e-mail message, click the **New Message** button. ■

> **Puzzled?**
>
> If you start Outlook using the New Message button (or a similar button), it displays the appropriate dialog box. After creating your new item, you're returned to the Windows desktop—*not* Outlook.

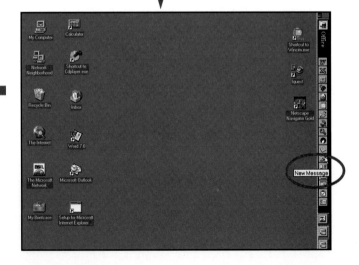

Switching Between the Outlook Programs

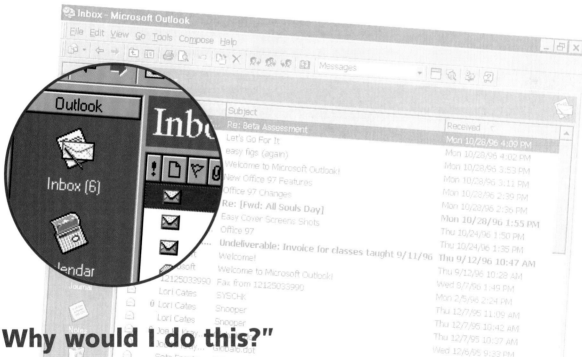

"Why would I do this?"

Before you can use any of the Outlook programs, you must first switch to it. When you switch to a program, the menu bar changes to display an extra menu which contains commands specific to that program. For example, when you change to the task list, the Tasks menu appears. In addition, some of the buttons on the Standard toolbar are replaced with buttons for commands you'd use only within the task list.

There are several methods you can use to switch from program to program in Outlook: the Outlook Bar, the Folder List, and the Go menu. In addition, you can use the Back and Forward buttons on the Standard toolbar. You'll learn how to use each of these in this task.

Task 2: Switching Between the Outlook Programs

1 When you use Outlook, it starts in the Inbox. To switch to another program, click its icon in the Outlook Bar, located on the left side of the window. For example, click the **Contacts** button.

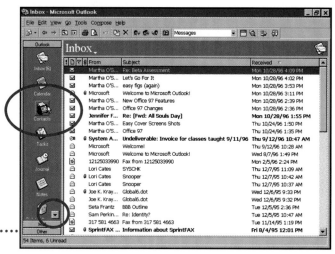

Puzzled?

If you don't see the icon for the program you want, click the **up** or **down arrow** within the Outlook bar.

2 Another way to change from one program to another in Outlook is by using the Folder List. To display the list, click the **Folder List** button on the Standard toolbar. To switch to a program, click its icon in the list. For example, click the Journal icon in the list. To hide the list, click the Folder List button again.

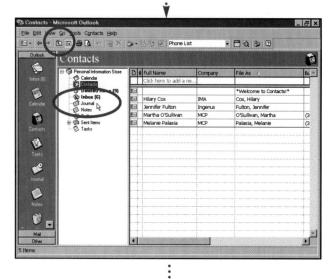

Puzzled?

If a folder contains subfolders, then it's proceeded by a small plus sign. To display the subfolders, click the plus sign. To hide them again, click the minus sign.

3 To display the Folder List, click the title of the current folder. For example, click the word, **Journal**, which appears at the top of the Journal window, and the Folder List appears. Click a folder in the list, and you change to that folder. For example, click **Inbox**. The Folder List then disappears.

Puzzled?

If you open the Folder list and decide not to switch to another folder, click outside the Folder list to remove it.

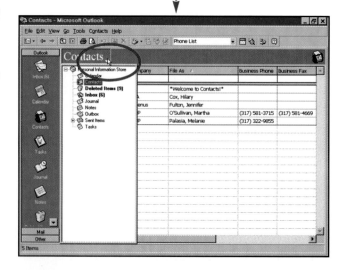

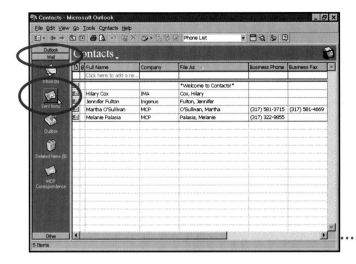

4 The Inbox displays e-mail messages you've received. To display a list of messages you've sent, you need to switch to the Mail section of Outlook. Click the **Mail** button at the bottom of the Outlook bar. The Mail button is moved to the top of the bar, and a list of mail-related icons is displayed. Click the **Sent Items** icon.

5 Another way to switch between Outlook programs is to use the Go menu. Click the **Go** menu to open it, then click the program to which you want to change, such as **Tasks**.

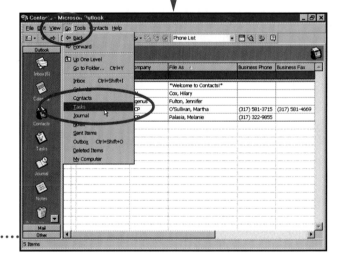

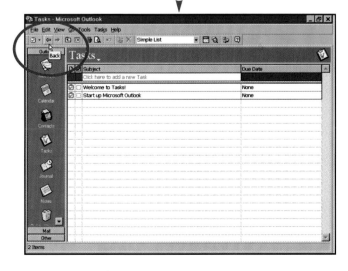

6 As you move from program to program in Outlook, it keeps track of your movements in a history file. You can move through this history by clicking the **Back** button on the Standard toolbar. For example, to return to the Sent Items folder, click the **Back** button. To return to the Tasks folder, click the **Forward** button. ■

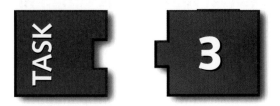

TASK 3

Getting to Know the Outlook Programs

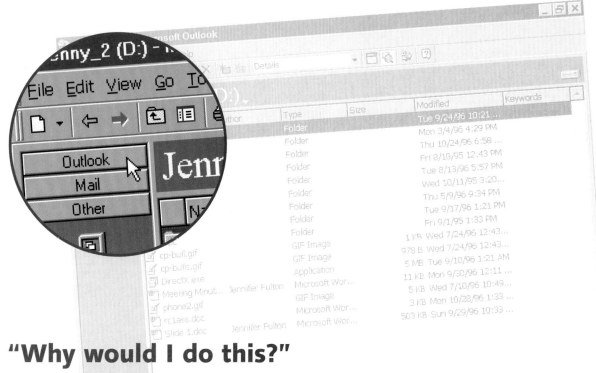

"Why would I do this?"

When you first start Outlook, it can be a bit confusing, because it's actually made up of several programs: Inbox, Calendar, Contacts, Tasks, Journal, and Notes.

Behind each of these strange sounding names is a powerful messaging system,

an appointment, meeting, and event planner; an address book; a task organizer; a business diary; and a notepad. Using Outlook will be difficult until you learn what each of these programs is for.

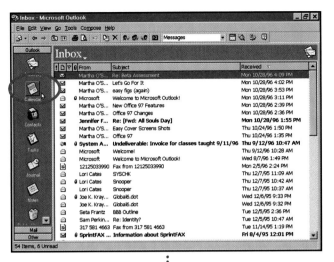

1 When you open Outlook for the first time, the Inbox is displayed. With the Inbox, you can check for e-mail messages, send an e-mail, send a fax, and plan a meeting. Click the **Calendar** icon.

Puzzled?

To set up Outlook to start with a different program instead of Inbox, open the **Tools** menu, select **Options**, and click the **General** tab. Then select the program you want to start with from the **Startup in this** drop-down list. Click **OK**.

2 With the Calendar, you can track appointments and plan meetings. You can make note of special events such as birthdays, anniversaries, and holidays. The Calendar can even remind you of important events, so you won't miss them. Click the **Contacts** icon.

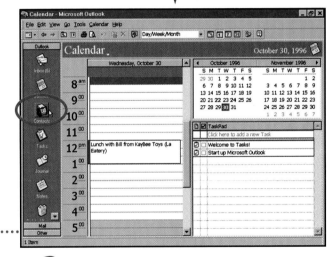

3 The Contacts list is like a big address book. Here you can keep track of business associates, family members, and friends, as well as their phone numbers, fax numbers, mobile phone numbers, e-mail addresses, and more. Click the **Tasks** icon.

Puzzled?

If you're switching to Outlook from a different electronic day planner, such as Schedule+ or Lotus Organizer, you can import your address book into Outlook without retyping it.

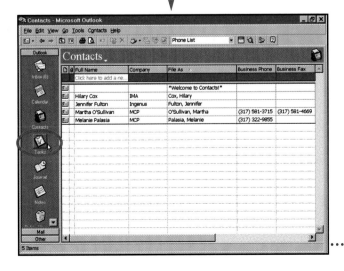

4 With the Tasks list, you can keep track of all those things you need to do. In addition, you can delegate a task to a co-worker and receive progress reports. Click the **Journal** icon.

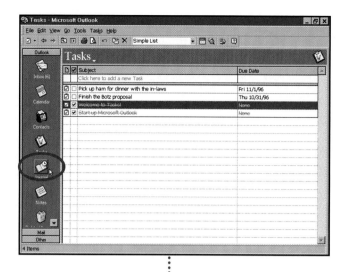

Missing Link

If you work with Outlook in a window that is not maximized, you might want to reduce the size of the icons on the Outlook bar. To do that, right-click any open space in the Outlook bar, then select **Small Icons** off the pop-up menu.

5 With the Journal, you can automatically track the Office documents you've worked on, and the dates on which you created or modified the documents. You can also track phone calls, conversations, and your thoughts in the Journal. Click the **Notes** icon.

Missing Link

Because the Journal tracks your document use, you can use it to open recently edited Office documents without having to remember exactly which drive and folder they're located on.

6 With Notes, you can jot a quick thought or idea. Click the **Deleted Items** icon. (You might need to click the **down** arrow on the Outlook bar to see the Deleted Items icon.)

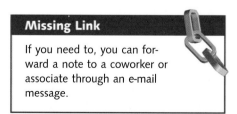

Missing Link

If you need to, you can forward a note to a coworker or associate through an e-mail message.

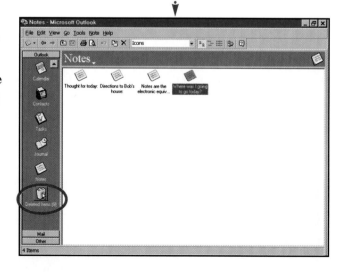

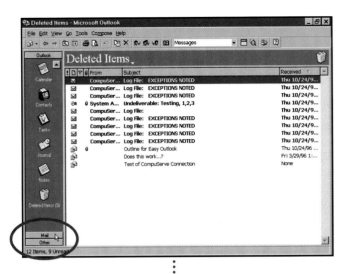

7 Deleted items are stored here temporarily (and not really deleted), until you tell Outlook to empty the contents of the Deleted Items bin. At that point, they are permanently removed from your system. Click the **Mail** button.

Puzzled?

To delete an item, click it and press **Delete**. If you want to delete all the items in your Deleted Items list, click **Edit**, then click **Select All**. Now press the **Delete** key.

8 The Mail group of icons provides access to e-mail related activities. The Inbox and Deleted Items icon are repeated here; they act the same as they did in the Outlook group of icons. New icons include the Sent Items icon (which contains copies of e-mail messages you've sent) and the Outbox (which contains messages waiting to be sent). Click the **Other** button.

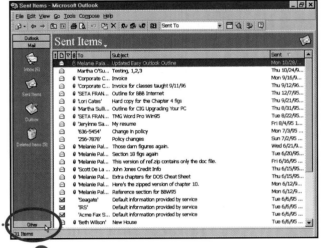

9 Here you can access the files on your computer or your company's network (through the My Computer icon). You can also access your Office Documents through the My Documents and My Favorites icons. To re-display the Outlook group of icons, click the **Outlook** button. ■

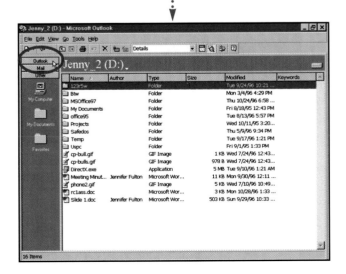

Puzzled?

You can add shortcuts to additional folders here, if needed. For example, if you keep project related files in a single folder, you could add that folder to this list.

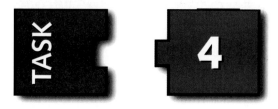

TASK **4**

Creating and Opening Your Documents from Within Outlook

"Why would I do this?"

Outlook provides quick access to your documents, which you'll often find convenient. For example, suppose you're working on an e-mail message and you want to include a copy of your sales worksheet, but you know that its figures are not current? No problem—you just switch to the Other group in the Outlook bar, locate the file on your PC or on your company's network, open the file, make your changes, and then insert the updated worksheet into your e-mail

message; all without actually leaving Outlook. You can even create new files with Office 97 from within Outlook.

You can also access recently used Office files from within your Journal—which eliminates the time it might take to locate them. Because hardly anyone works in a single program at a time, it makes sense that you can launch other programs and open documents with a simple click from within Outlook.

20

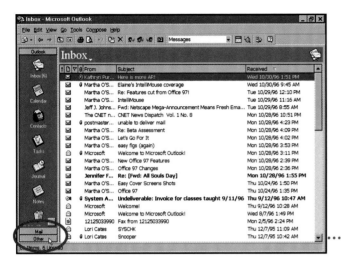

1 On the Outlook bar, click the **Other** button. The Other group of icons is displayed.

2 Click **My Computer**, and the contents of your PC is displayed. Select a drive from the list and double-click it to see a listing of the files on that drive. To create a new Office document, skip to Step 4. To open an existing document, double-click a folder, and continue with Step 3.

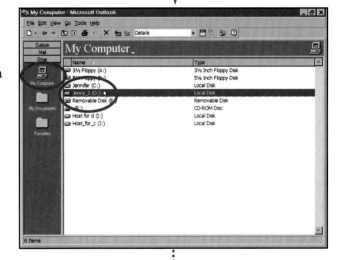

Puzzled?

If you save your Office files in the My Documents or My Favorites folders (a common practice), click one of those icons instead. A listing of files in that folder appears.

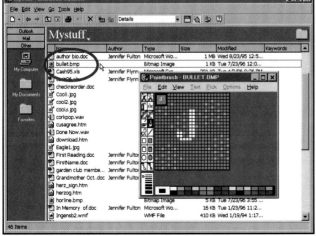

3 To edit an existing file, just double-click it. The program that created the file opens, displaying the contents of the file you selected. Make your changes, and then skip to Step 6.

Puzzled?

If you can't locate your file, you can have Outlook search for it. See Task 65 for help.

Task 4: Creating and Opening Your Documents from Within Outlook

4 You can start a new Office 97 document from within any part of Outlook. Just open the **File** menu, select **New**, and then select **Office Document**.

Missing Link

To display the complete list of Office templates, as seen in Step 5, perform this step while in My Computer.

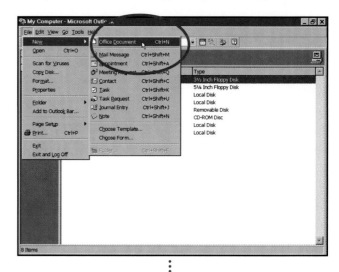

5 In the New Office Document dialog box, click the tab of the document type you want to create, then click the template you want to use. Click **OK**. The Office program associated with that template starts. Complete the template to finish.

Puzzled?

A *template*, is a semi-completed document of a particular type. Office provides templates for common documents such as letters, expense reports the memos.

6 After completing your document, click the **Save** button. To return to Outlook, open the **File** menu and select **Exit**.

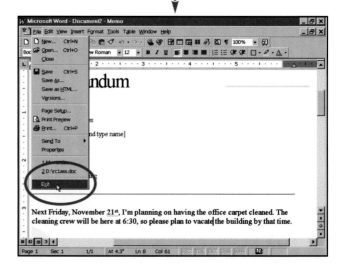

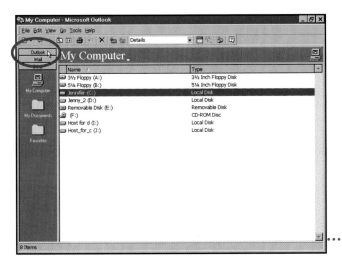

7 If the file you want to edit is an Office 97 file and you've used it recently, chances are you'll find it in the Journal. Click the **Outlook** button on the Outlook bar.

8 Click the **Journal** icon to display the contents of the Journal. Use the scrollbars to locate your file. Double-click the file. A journal window opens.

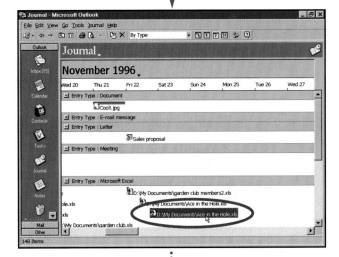

Puzzled?

If you'd like to bypass the journal window and open the file immediately when you double-click it, open the Tools menu, select Options, then click the Journal tab. Select the **Opens the item referred to by the journal entry** option, then click **OK**.

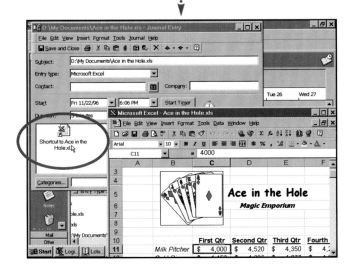

9 Double-click the shortcut icon to open the file and make your changes. When you're through, save the file, then open the **File** menu and select **Exit** to return to Outlook. ■

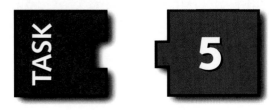

Adjusting the Size of Columns

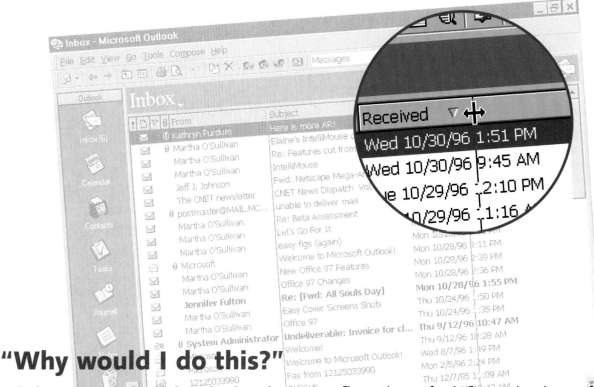

"Why would I do this?"

Information in Outlook is displayed in columns. For example, when you view your e-mail messages in the Inbox, information about each message is displayed in several columns, such as the name of the person who sent the message, its subject, the date when the message was received, and so on.

Sometimes the information in a column is not displayed completely, because the column is too small. In this task, you'll learn how to adjust the size of your columns so you can see the information you need.

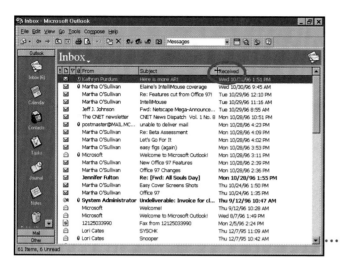

1 Move the mouse pointer over the right edge of the column you want to adjust. The pointer changes to a vertical line crossed by two arrows.

2 Press and hold the mouse button down. Drag the border to the right to make the column wider; drag the border to the left to make the column smaller.

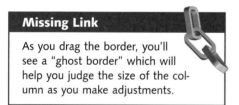

Missing Link

As you drag the border, you'll see a "ghost border" which will help you judge the size of the column as you make adjustments.

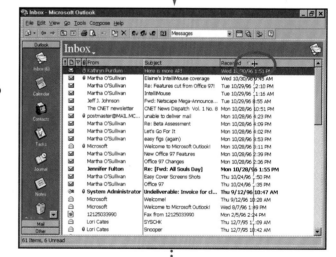

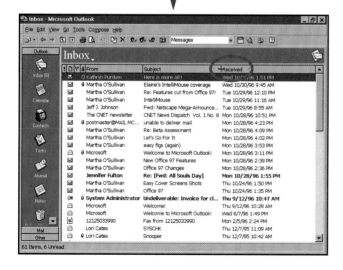

3 If you want to make a column the width of its longest item, just position the mouse pointer over the column's right edge and double-click. ■

TASK

6

Changing Views and How Information Is Sorted

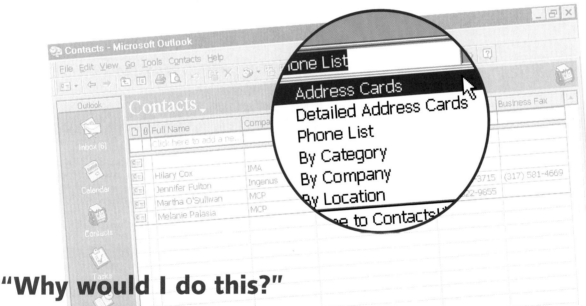

"Why would I do this?"

Each of Outlook's programs displays its information in a particular way. You can change the way in which information is displayed by changing the view. For example, the items in the Contacts list are typically displayed as a phone list, with each person and his phone numbers shown on a separate line. You can change to a different view if you want. For example, you could select a view that displays each person's phone numbers and e-mail addresses in a card format.

You can also change the order in which information is displayed. Items in each Outlook section are always sorted in a particular order. For example, the items in the Inbox are sorted by the date they are received, from the most recent message to the oldest. You can reverse the order of how information is displayed or you can change the column by which the information is sorted. For example, you can have items sorted by the received date or by the name of the person who sent them.

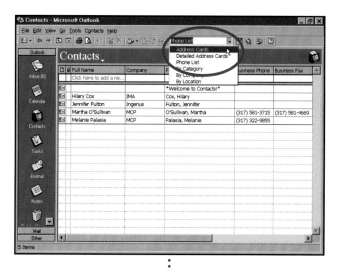

1 To change to a different view, open the **Current View** list on the Standard toolbar and select the view you want. For example, the Contacts list initially displays each item on a separate line. To display the items in a card format, select **Address Cards** from the Current View list.

Puzzled?

If you select a view you don't like, simply open the **Current View** list, and select a different view.

2 To reverse the order of how items are sorted, click the button marked by the arrow. In the Inbox, click the **Received** button to reverse the sort order.

Missing Link

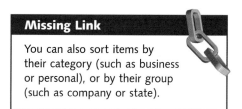

You can also sort items by their category (such as business or personal), or by their group (such as company or state).

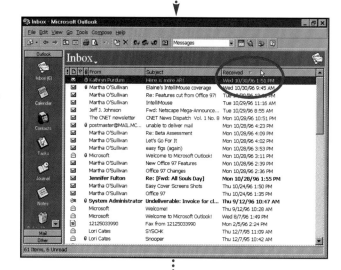

3 To sort by a different column (field), click that column's header (title) instead. For example, click the **From** header, and the items in the Inbox are sorted by the person who sent them. ■

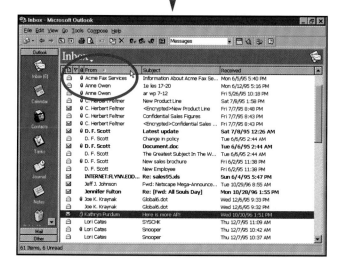

Missing Link

You may be able to display a preview pane at the bottom of the Inbox Window. See Task 10.

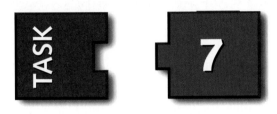

Using the Office Assistant to Get Help

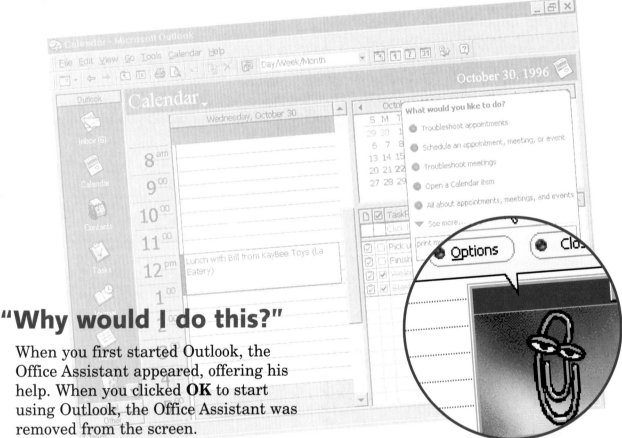

"Why would I do this?"

When you first started Outlook, the Office Assistant appeared, offering his help. When you clicked **OK** to start using Outlook, the Office Assistant was removed from the screen.

If you later run up against a wall and can't figure out how to perform a particular task in Outlook, you can call on the Office Assistant and ask for his help. With the Office Assistant, you simply type your question just as you would ask it of a colleague—for example, **How do I exit the program?** The Assistant responds with a listing of possible answers, from which you can choose. Each answer provides detailed steps for completing some procedure.

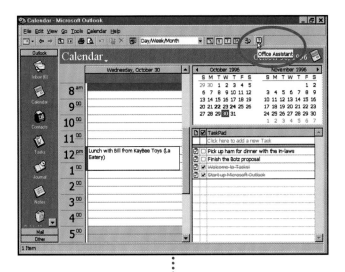

1 When you first start Outlook, the Office Assistant appears, offering its help. To display the Assistant at a later time, click the **Office Assistant** button on the Standard toolbar.

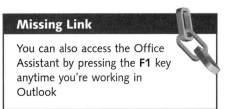

Missing Link

You can also access the Office Assistant by pressing the **F1** key anytime you're working in Outlook

2 The Office Assistant enables you to get information using a question format. Type your question in the text box, and then click **Search**.

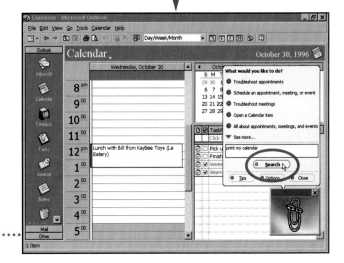

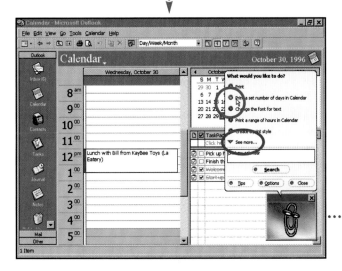

3 A list of available topics related to your question appears. Click the topic which best suits your needs.

Missing Link

To see additional topics, click **See more**. If you click See more, and want to return to the previous listing, click **See previous**.

4 A list of steps describing how to complete that procedure appears. Follow the steps on-screen, then click the **Close** button (the **X**) to return to Outlook. Some topics include a **Show me** button. Click this button, and Outlook shows you how to complete each step.

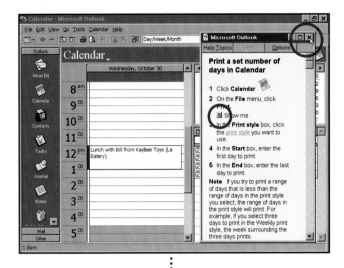

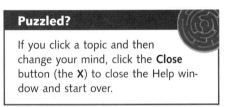

Puzzled?

If you click a topic and then change your mind, click the **Close** button (the **X**) to close the Help window and start over.

5 The Office Assistant remains on-screen. When you have another question, simply click its title bar, and the text box into which you type your question appears. To remove the Office Assistant from the screen, click the **Close** button (the **X**).

6 Sometimes, based on your current task, the Office Assistant has a suggestion to make. At that time, a small light bulb will appear on the **Office Assistant** button. To see the suggestion, click the Office Assistant button to display the Office Assistant window (if the Office Assistant is already displayed, skip this step).

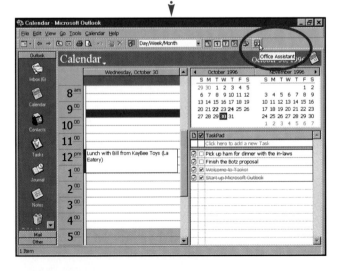

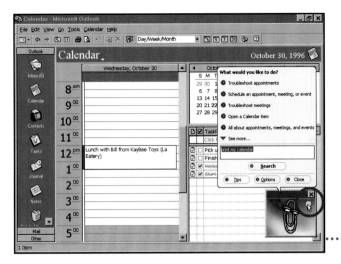

7 In the Office Assistant box, click the light bulb. A suggestion appears.

8 Read the suggestion and then click **Close** to remove the suggestion box from the screen. ■

Missing Link

You can click **Back** in the suggestion box to see a previous suggestion. After clicking **Back**, the Next button will no longer appear grayed, which means that you can click it to move forward through the suggestion list.

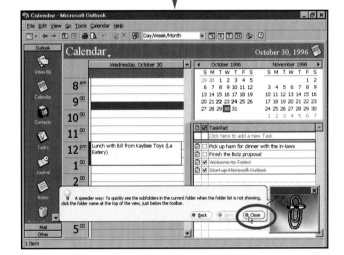

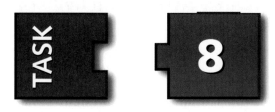

TASK 8

Exiting Microsoft Outlook

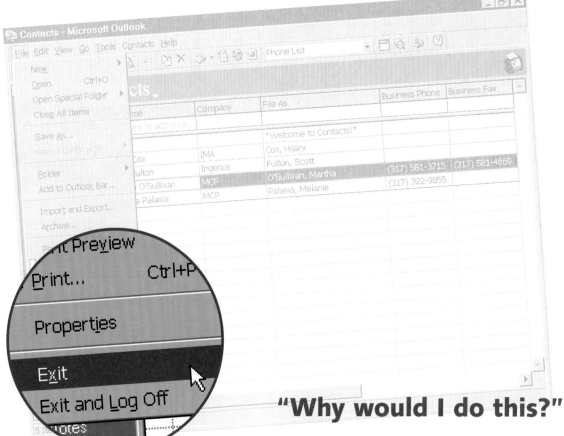

"Why would I do this?"

When you finish working in Outlook, you need to leave the program. Correctly exiting any program means learning the right way to exit; if you just turn off the computer when you finish working, you lose any unsaved data and run the risk of damaging other files.

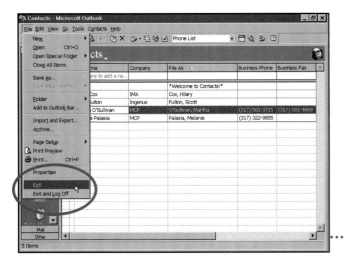

1 Open the **File** menu and choose **Exit**. You're returned to the Windows desktop.

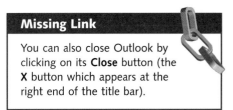

Missing Link

You can also close Outlook by clicking on its **Close** button (the **X** button which appears at the right end of the title bar).

2 If you're logged into a messaging service such as the Internet or CompuServe, select **Exit and Log Off** instead. This command logs you off the messaging service and exits Outlook.

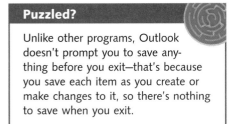

Puzzled?

Unlike other programs, Outlook doesn't prompt you to save anything before you exit—that's because you save each item as you create or make changes to it, so there's nothing to save when you exit.

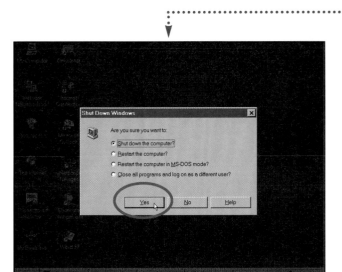

3 From the Windows 95 desktop, you can continue working with other programs or shut down your computer. To shut down the computer, click the **Start** button on the taskbar. The Start menu appears. Click **Shut Down**, and you'll see the Shut Down Windows dialog box. Here, click **Shut down the computer?** and click **Yes**. In a minute or two, you see the message **It's now safe to turn off your computer.** When you see that message, turn off the computer. ■

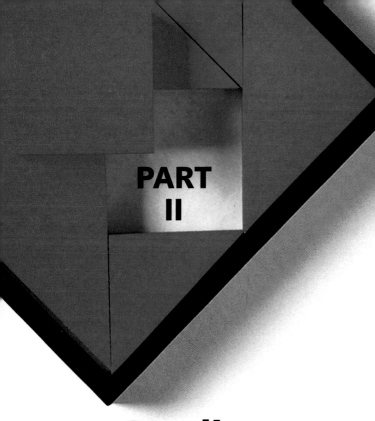

PART II

Sending, Receiving, and Managing Electronic Mail with Inbox

Y OU CAN USE OUTLOOK TO SEND AND RECEIVE E-MAIL MESSAGES. To send a message to someone, you'll need his or her e-mail address.

The process of creating your message is similar to using a word processor, although much simpler. You type your text, format it (add bold, italics, underline, and so on), correct any typing errors, then send it. If you have Microsoft Word installed, you can use it as your editor—although you don't have to. But using Word means you can take advantage of its advanced features such as automatic spell-checking, table handling, bulleted and numbered lists.

You can attach a file to the message if you like, and send it along with the message text. You can also attach items you create with Outlook's other programs, such as Journal or Notes.

If you access the World Wide Web often, and you wish to share some special source of information, you can include the address of your favorite Web sites in a message. When your coworker opens your message, he or she can connect to the Internet and use the addresses you included to visit the sites you mentioned. The addresses appear as hypertext links, so all your coworker needs to do (after connecting to the Internet, of course) is to click on the link to view the particular Web page to which it refers.

An Internet e-mail address is composed of several segments. For example, the address **jsmith@hr.cooper.com** can be broken down like this: the first part (**jsmith**) is the name by which the recipient is known on his mail system. This might be the person's real name or a nickname. An @ sign always follows the user's name. The last part (**hr.cooper.com**) is the name of the Internet server PC which handles J. Smith's mail. The **hr** might refer to Human

Resources, and the **cooper** might be the name of the company he works for. The last part, **.com**, tells you that this is a commercial (business) Internet site, as opposed to **.mil** (military), **.org** (nonprofit organization), **.edu** (educational), or **.gov** (government), to name a few.

If you want to send a message through the Internet to someone who uses some other messaging service such as CompuServe or AOL, then the process is a bit more complicated. Use the following as a guide for creating the Internet address you need:

Service	User's Address	Internet Address
CompuServe	71354,1254	71354.1254@ compuserve.com
America Online	joemsmith	joemsmith@aol.com
Prodigy	joemsmith	joemsmith@prodigy.com
Microsoft Network	flyboy	flyboy@msn.com

You can also add voting buttons to a message. This enables you to type a message such as "Would you like to work 1 hour extra every day this week in order to get off early on Friday?" which you could send to all your coworkers, complete with the buttons "Yes" and "No" with which they could answer your question. When the recipient reads the message and clicks one of the buttons, a response is sent to your system where it can be automatically tabulated by Outlook. The buttons of course, are not limited to a simple Yes or No—for example, you could ask your coworkers to vote on several different medical plan options, etc.

Another thing that is nice to include with an e-mail message is an AutoSignature. Basically, this is a file with the text with which you normally close your messages. For example, an AutoSignature might include your name, phone number, and e-mail address—any text which you normally include with your messages.

Adding a Messaging Service

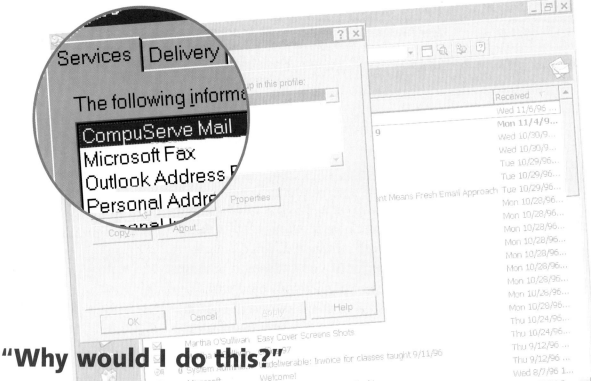

"Why would I do this?"

Before you can use Inbox, you must install the messaging services you wish to use. A messaging service collects and sends electronic mail for the users who subscribe to the service. Popular messaging services include the Internet, CompuServe, Microsoft Network, America Online, and Prodigy, to name a few. Also, if your company has a network and you use Microsoft Mail or cc:Mail, you can send your e-mail messages through Outlook.

Some messaging services are easy to add to Outlook, since they are installed when Outlook itself is installed. These include cc:Mail, Microsoft Network, Microsoft Mail, Microsoft Exchange Server (which handles mail on a Windows NT network), and the Microsoft at Work fax program (for sending faxes through a fax machine attached to your company's network). To add other messaging services, you'll need that service's program disks.

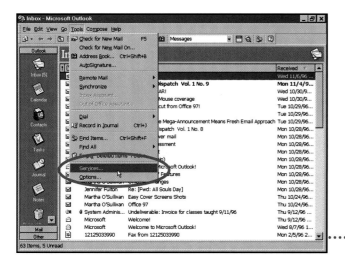

1 Open the **Tools** menu and select **Services**.

2 The services which you've already installed are listed in the Services dialog box. If you used to use Microsoft Exchange, then the services you installed there appear here automatically. To add a new service, click **Add**.

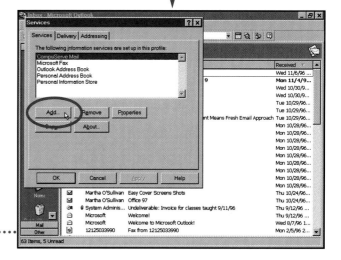

3 In the Add Service to Profile dialog box, select the service you wish to use from those listed under **Available information services**, and click **OK**.

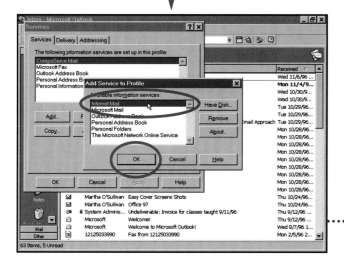

> **Puzzled?**
>
> If your service is not listed, you will need its software to install it. Click **Have Disk**, then select the service's setup program, and click **OK** to install it. The service will be added to the list of those available. Select it and click **OK**.

4 What you see in this step will vary based on the service you're trying to install. Enter your name, e-mail address, and other information you receive from your Internet service provider. Click the **Connection** tab.

Puzzled?

If you don't know some of the information, call your Internet Service provider.

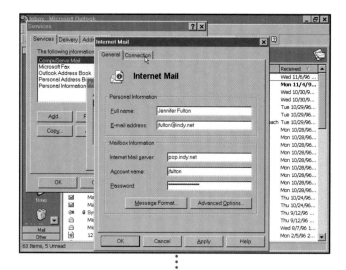

5 On the **Connection** tab, select how you plan to connect to the Internet; if you use a modem, you may want to select **Work off-line and use Remote Mail**, in order to stop Outlook from trying to check for e-mail when you're not connected to the Internet. Click **OK**.

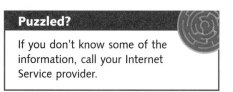

Missing Link

The Exit and Log Off command on the File menu can be used to exit Outlook and log off of a messaging service at the same time.

6 You'll see a message saying that you cannot use your new service until you restart Outlook. Click **OK**, and you're returned to the Services dialog box. Click **OK**, and you're returned to Outlook.

7 To exit Outlook, open **File** and select **Exit**. Click **Start**, select **Programs**, and then select **Microsoft Outlook**. ■

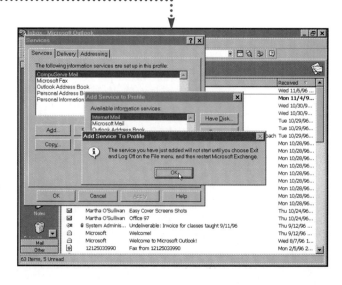

Creating and Sending a Message

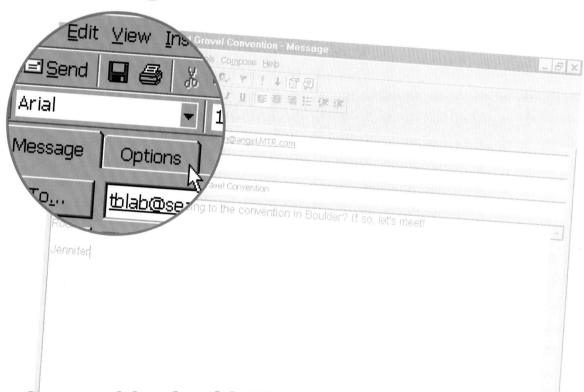

"Why would I do this?"

Electronic mail (e-mail for short) is a convenient and quick way to keep in contact with those people who are the most important to you. Unlike a letter which may take days to reach its recipient, an e-mail message takes only minutes on a local network (or, through the Internet or some other messaging service, it might take a few hours). Also, unlike a conventional letter, an e-mail message can contain other information in the form of files: a client database, a budget spreadsheet, or a sales chart (graph). You can send e-mail messages easily with Inbox.

1 Click the **New Mail Message** button on the Standard toolbar. The Message window appears.

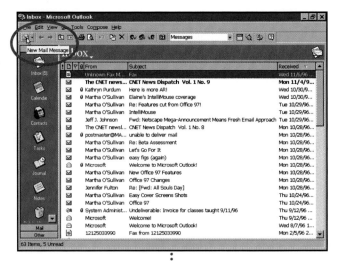

Puzzled?

The New button changes functions to display the last command you used. If the words New Mail Message do not appear as you point to the button with the mouse pointer, then click the down arrow and select it from the new list.

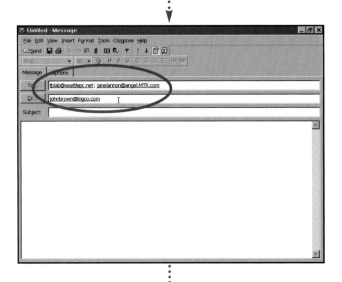

2 In the **To** text box, type the address of the person to whom you wish to send your message. To add a second person's name, type a semicolon first (**;**), then type the additional address. To send a copy of the message to someone else, enter an address in the **Cc** text box instead. Click in the **Subject** box or press **Tab** to move the cursor.

3 Type the subject of your message in the **Subject** box. Click in the text box or press **Tab** to move the cursor there.

Puzzled?

If for some reason, the Cc and Subject text boxes are not visible, click the **Message Header** button on the Standard toolbar to display them.

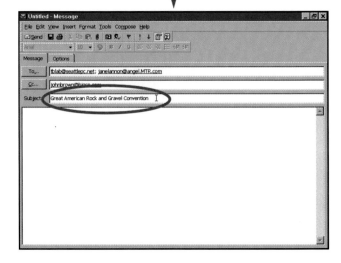

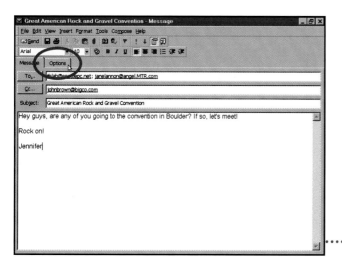

4 Type your message in the big text box. To set options for how the message is delivered, click the **Options** tab.

Missing Link

Messages, after they've been sent, are placed in the Sent folder. You can select a different folder, by clicking the **Browse** button and selecting one from the list.

5 Within the General options section, set the level of importance (high priority, low priority) with the **Importance** list. You can select the level of **Sensitivity** as well (Normal, Private, and Confidential). You can have replies to messages sent to someone else by typing their address in the **Have replies sent to** text box.

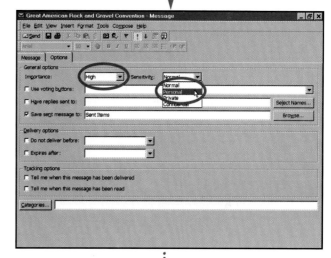

Missing Link

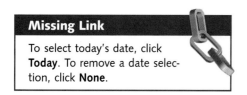

To select today's date, click **Today**. To remove a date selection, click **None**.

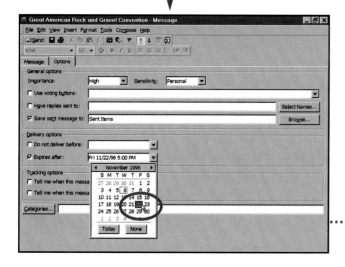

6 In the **Delivery** options section, you can set the date when you want the message delivered, and an expiration date as well. This will prevent the message from being delivered *after* a particular date. Click the down arrow and a calendar appears. Click the left or right arrows at the top of the calendar to move from month to month, then click the date you want.

7 To have a message sent back to you, choose one of the options in the Tracking options area.

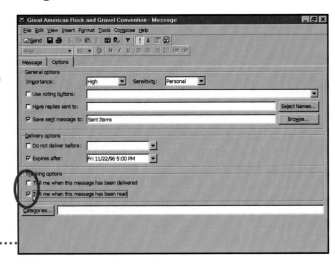

Missing Link

By clicking the **Categories** button, you can select a category for this message.

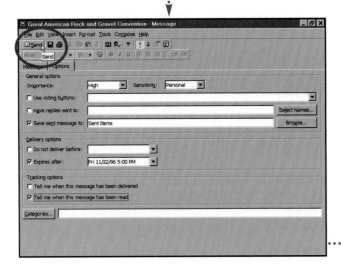

8 To send the message, turn on your modem (if needed) and click the **Send** button. (If your message is not yet finished but you'd like to save it to send later, open the **File** menu and select **Save**.) Outlook connects to your messaging service and sends the message. After a message is sent, it is placed in the Sent folder, which you can access through the Mail button on the Outlook bar.

9 If your message was not sent automatically, you can send it manually by simply checking for new messages. Open the **Tools** menu and select **Check for New Mail On**.

10 In the Check for New Mail On dialog box, select the services for which you want to check (or send) messages, then click **OK**. ■

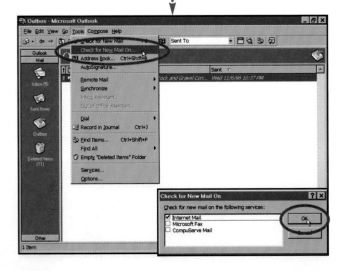

Using Templates

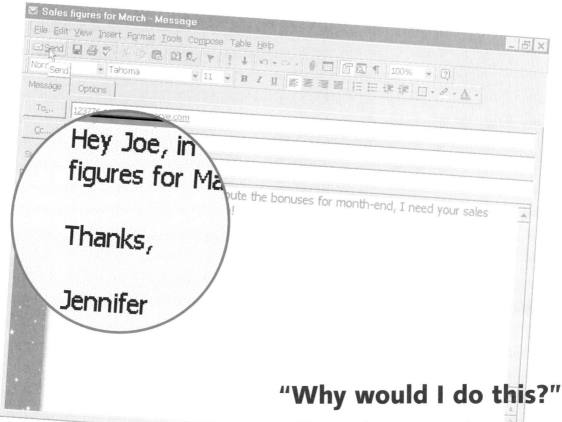

"Why would I do this?"

The templates you use for creating mail messages are actually part of Word 97. If you used a standard installation to install Office 97, Word templates will be available to you.

There is one catch, however: you must have Microsoft Word installed in order to use the templates.

Task 11: Using Templates

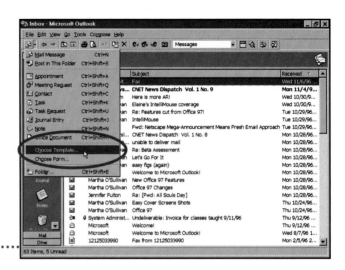

1 Click the **arrow** on the **New** button located on the Standard toolbar. A list of commands appears; select **Choose Template** from this list.

2 In the Choose Template dialog box, click a template icon and click **OK**. For example, click the Midnight icon.

> **Puzzled?**
>
> Some of the templates listed are for creating other Outlook items, such as appointments, contacts, tasks, and blank e-mail messages.

3 A message window opens with the template you choose. If you selected the Midnight template, you'll notice a field of stars on the left edge of the message area, and a unique font for your text. Enter an address in the **To** box, a **Subject**, and your message. Then click **Send**. ■

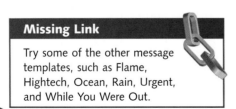

> **Missing Link**
>
> Try some of the other message templates, such as Flame, Hightech, Ocean, Rain, Urgent, and While You Were Out.

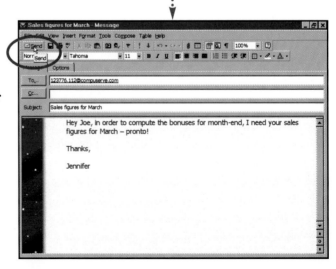

Formatting Text

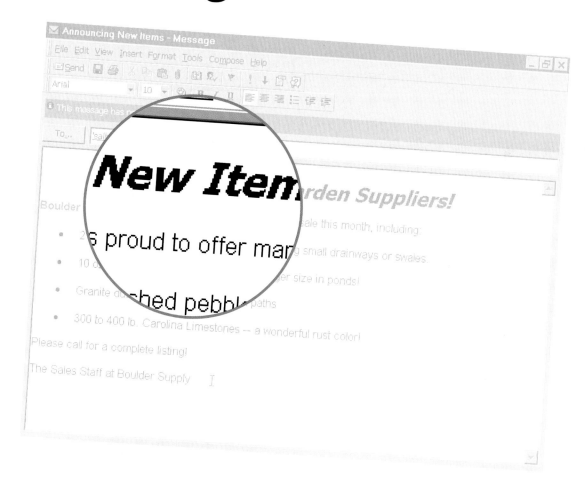

"Why would I do this?"

To add emphasis to the words in your message, you can format them. With formatting, you can add bold, italics, or underline. In addition, you can change the font (typestyle), size, color, or alignment of your text. You can even create bulleted lists (a list of items, each of which is preceded by a small bullet, or dot). When you apply formatting, you can change all the text in your message, or selected text.

Task 12: Formatting Text

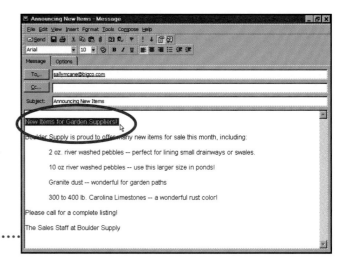

1 In the message area, select the text you wish to change. To select text, click at the beginning of the text, then press and hold the mouse button as you drag the mouse pointer to the end of the text. The text you select is highlighted.

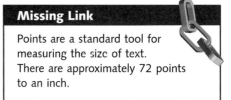

2 If you want, select a font from the **Font** list. The selected text is changed to that typestyle. To change the size of the selected text, select a point size from the **Font Size** list.

Missing Link

Points are a standard tool for measuring the size of text. There are approximately 72 points to an inch.

3 To change the color of the selected text, click the **Font Color** button, then select a color from the list.

Puzzled?

If you select a color you don't like, select a different one, or open the **Edit** menu and choose **Undo**.

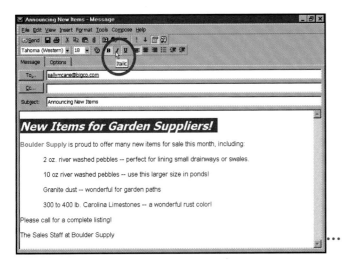

4 You can add bold, italic, or underline to the selected text by clicking the **Bold**, **Italic**, or **Underline** buttons on the Formatting toolbar.

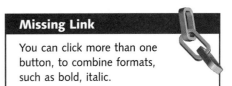

Missing Link

You can click more than one button, to combine formats, such as bold, italic.

5 To change the alignment of the selected text, click the **Align Left**, **Center**, or **Align Right** buttons.

Missing Link

An *indent* is simply additional space (usually five spaces) which is added to the left margin, in order to increase the amount of space between the text and the left edge of the page.

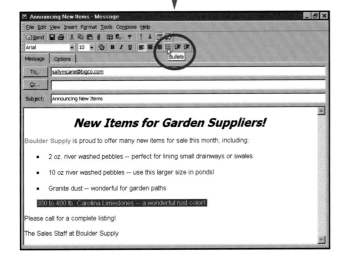

6 To add bullets in front of items in a list, select the list of items to be bulleted, then click the **Bullets** button. To move the text farther from the left margin, click the **Increase Indent** button. Each time you click, additional space (indents) are added between the selected text and the margin. To remove an indent, click the **Decrease Indent** button, and the text moves closer to the left margin. ■

TASK 13

Attaching a File to a Message

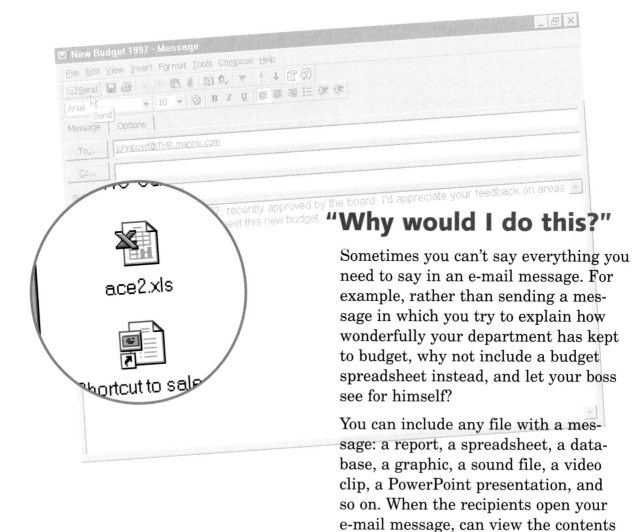

"Why would I do this?"

Sometimes you can't say everything you need to say in an e-mail message. For example, rather than sending a message in which you try to explain how wonderfully your department has kept to budget, why not include a budget spreadsheet instead, and let your boss see for himself?

You can include any file with a message: a report, a spreadsheet, a database, a graphic, a sound file, a video clip, a PowerPoint presentation, and so on. When the recipients open your e-mail message, can view the contents of the file (provided they have a program capable of reading the information), or they can save the file to their hard disk.

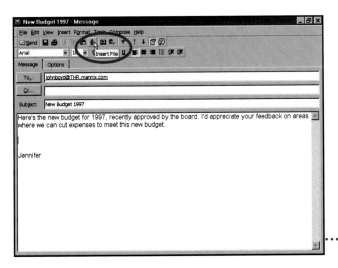

1 After you type the text for your message, click the **Insert File** button on the Standard toolbar. The Insert File dialog box appears.

2 Locate the drive and folder in which the file exists, then double-click the folder. To move up one level, click the **Up One Level** button. To change to a different drive, select that drive from the **Look in** list. Once the file you want is visible, click it.

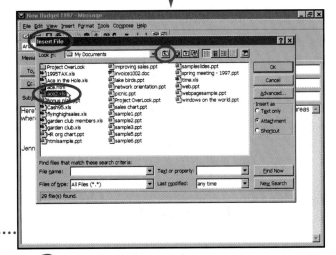

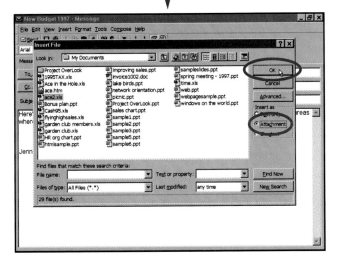

3 To provide a link to the file, click the **Shortcut** option under Insert as. To include the information as text, select **Text only**. Otherwise, leave the option set at **Attachment**. Click **OK** to insert the file or link. Click **Send** to send your message. ■

Missing Link

If you attached the file to the message in Step 3, then the file appears as an icon within the message. If you included a shortcut to the file instead, then it appears as a short-cut icon.

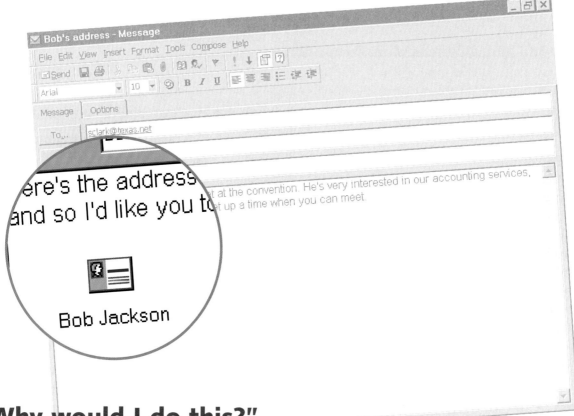

Attaching an Outlook Item

"Why would I do this?"

In addition to being able to attach files to your messages, you can attach Outlook items as well. For example, you might attach a Journal entry, or a particular contact, or task item to share with a colleague.

If you wish to share an e-mail message, you do not attach it to another message—instead, you simply *forward* it (something which you'll learn to do in an upcoming task).

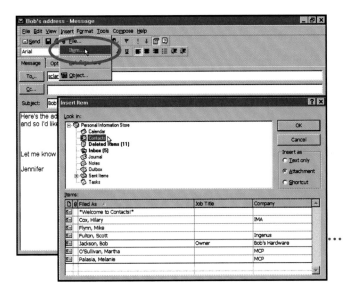

1 After you type the text for your message, open the **Insert** menu and select **Item**.

2 In the **Look in** list, click the Outlook folder which contains the item you want to insert. The contents of that folder appear in the **Items** window below.

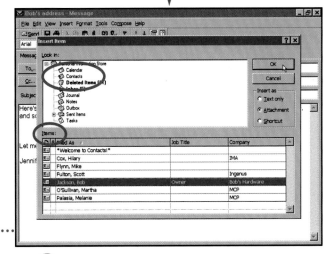

3 Click the item you want to insert. If you'd like to insert the item as text, then select **Text only** from the Insert as list. (For example, if the recipient doesn't use Outlook.) To insert it as a shortcut, select the **Shortcut** option instead. When you're ready, click **OK** to insert the item. ■

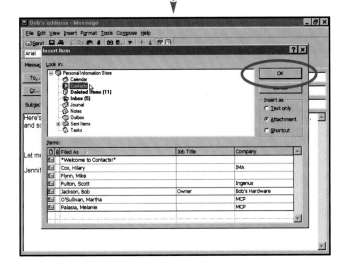

Missing Link

You can also insert an item by simply dragging it into an open message, or (to create a new message) by dragging it onto the Inbox folder.

53

Adding Voting Buttons

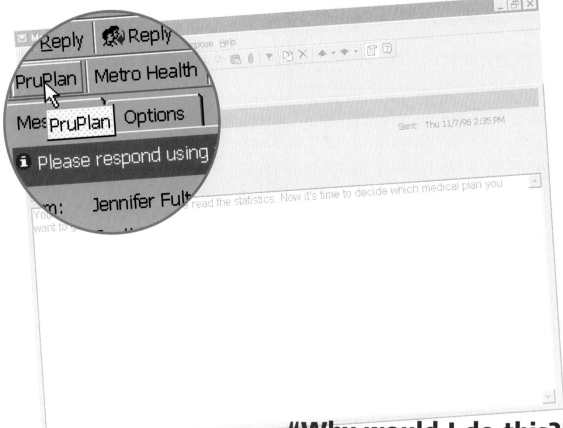

"Why would I do this?"

You can attach voting buttons to a message, and your recipients can then vote on various propositions, such as a salary cut, a benefits change, and so on.

The buttons look the same as those you'd find in a dialog box. When the user opens your message, he simply clicks the button of his choice, and a reply is sent back to you.

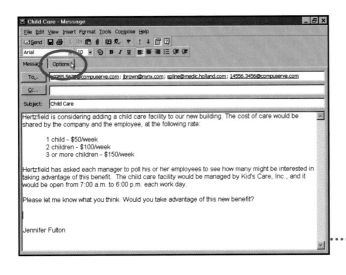

1 After typing the text of your message, click the **Options** tab.

2 Select the **Use voting buttons** option, then select the button names you want to use from the list.

Puzzled?

If you want to assign your own names to the voting buttons, then just type them in the text box, separated by semicolons, like this: Plan A; Plan B; Plan C. There is no limit to the number of voting buttons you can use.

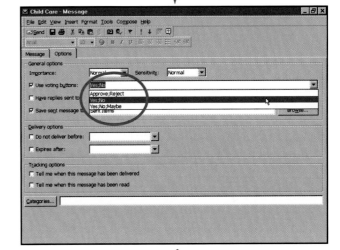

3 When you're ready, click **Send** to send your e-mail message.

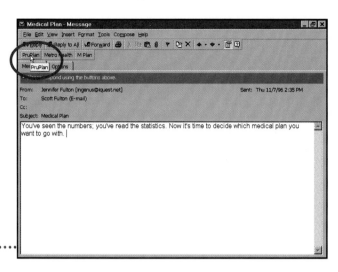

4 If you receive an e-mail message in which you're asked to respond, open that message by double-clicking it. You'll see voting buttons on a toolbar at the top of the window. To respond to the query, simply click the button of your choice.

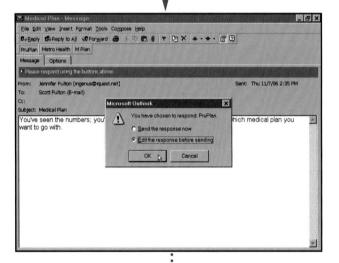

5 A dialog box appears. Click **Send the response now** to send your voting response. If you want to send a comment in the form of an e-mail message, click **Edit the response before sending** instead. Then click **OK**.

Missing Link

If someone sent a comment with a response, then his response was recorded in the Tracking list and the comment was placed in the Inbox as a regular e-mail message. Switch to the Inbox to view any comments.

6 To review the responses to a question you've sent, switch to the **Sent** folder and open your original message by double-clicking it. You'll find an extra tab called **Tracking**. Click it to view a summary of the responses to your query, which appears at the top of the window. ■

Adding a Web Shortcut

"Why would I do this?"

If you use the Internet and your colleagues do too, why not share with them the locations of Web sites which you've found useful? Outlook allows you to easily include an Internet address (or URL) to your message. The address appears as an icon, which, when clicked, takes the user to the associated Web site. Now, in order for the recipients of your message to use the address you include, must have a Web browser such as Internet Explorer or Netscape, and an Internet connection. In order to add the address to the e-mail message, you simply insert it from your bookmark or Favorites list—the list within your Web browser where you store your favorite Web addresses. If the address you want to insert is not on your bookmark list, you can simply type it into the e-mail message by hand.

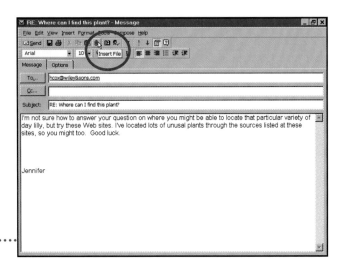

1 Type the text for your message. Then, if you use Internet Explorer, click the **Insert File** button on the Standard toolbar. If you use a different Web browser such as Netscape, then skip to Step 4.

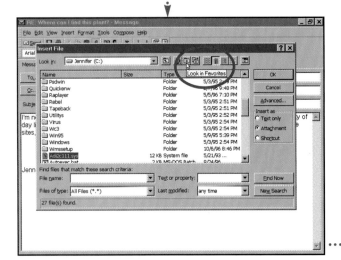

2 Click the **Look in Favorites** button at the top of the window.

3 Open the folder in which you store your bookmarks, then click the icon for the Web page whose address you want to include in your e-mail message. Click **OK**, and the address is inserted into the message as an icon.

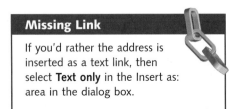

Missing Link

If you'd rather the address is inserted as a text link, then select **Text only** in the Insert as: area in the dialog box.

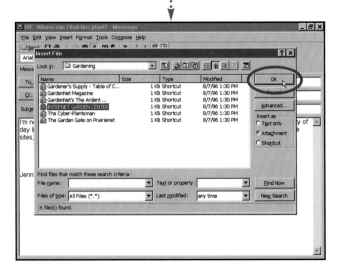

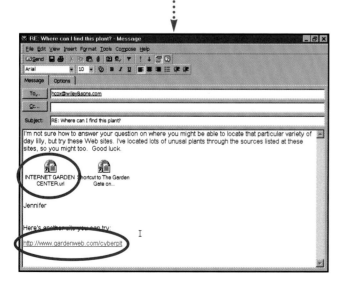

4 If you use another Web browser, such as Netscape, then you need to start that program, and open the Bookmarks window. In Netscape, you can do that by opening the **Bookmarks** list and selecting **Go to Bookmarks**.

Puzzled?

You don't need to connect to the Internet at this time; simply start the Netscape program (or whatever Web browser you use).

5 If needed, resize the Bookmarks window so you can see it as well as your e-mail message. Then click the bookmark you want to insert, and drag it into the message window. When you release the mouse button, the address of the Web page you selected is inserted as an icon.

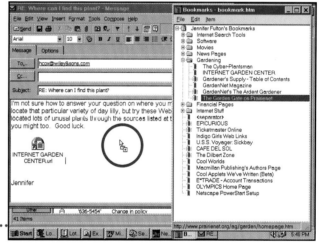

6 If the address you want to insert is not in your bookmarks list, then simply type the address manually into the text of your message. The text you type is converted to a hypertext link—blue, underlined text. When it's clicked, it takes the user to the indicated Web address. ■

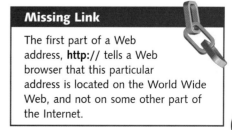

Missing Link

The first part of a Web address, **http://** tells a Web browser that this particular address is located on the World Wide Web, and not on some other part of the Internet.

TASK **17**

Adding an AutoSignature

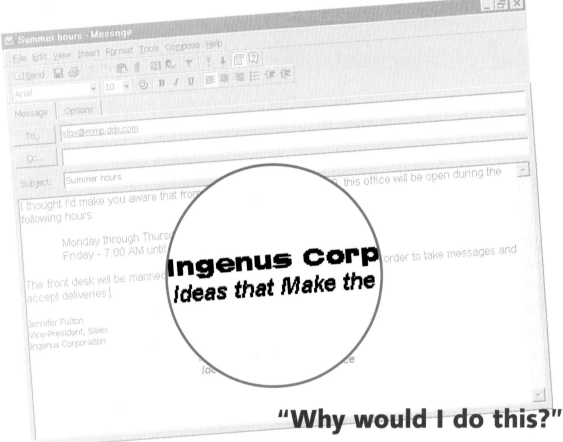

"Why would I do this?"

An AutoSignature is a text file which you can insert into your messages. You might include your name, company, e-mail address, and other pertinent information you want to include with your messages on a regular basis.

By creating an AutoSignature file, you can simply insert this information instead of retyping it each time you want to create a new message.

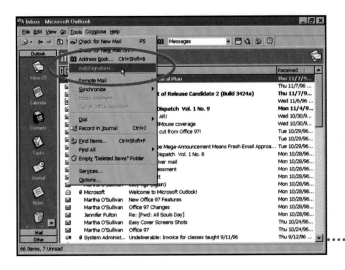

1 If needed, change to the Inbox. Then open the **Tools** menu and select **AutoSignature**. The AutoSignature dialog box appears.

2 Type the text you want to use as your AutoSignature into the text box.

Puzzled?

You can change the font of text and add attributes by clicking the **Font** button and making your selections. If you want to change the alignment of text (such as centering it), click the **Paragraph** button and make your selection. You can add bullets to list items with the Paragraph button.

3 If you want your AutoSignature to be automatically included in each message you create, then click the **Add this signature to the end of new messages** option. If you do not want your AutoSignature included in messages which you reply to, or forward, then click the **Don't add this signature to replies or forwarded messages** option to deselect it. ■

TASK

18

Checking Spelling

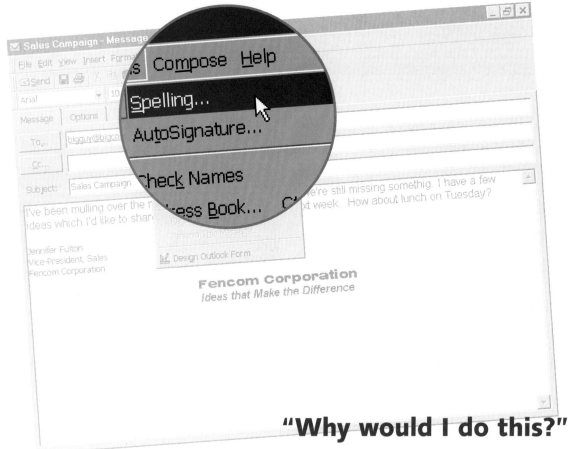

"Why would I do this?"

Everyone makes typographical and spelling errors at one time or another, but it would be a shame to let these errors ruin your message. Fortunately, Outlook's spell-checking utility and built-in dictionary make it easy to find and fix your spelling errors. Outlook even enables you to add your own words to its built-in dictionary.

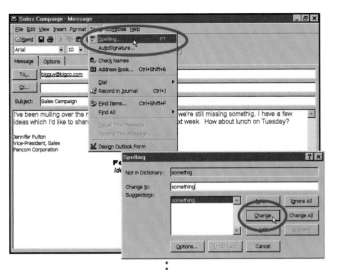

1 Type the text of your message. To check for errors, open the **Tools** menu and select **Spelling**. This starts the spell-checking utility, which will locate your errors.

Missing Link

Check the spelling of a single word or a group of words by selecting the text *before* you select the **Spelling** command. If you don't select any text, the utility checks the entire message.

2 When the spell-checking utility finds a word that is not in its dictionary, it displays the misspelled word and other suggested spellings in the Spelling dialog box. Select a suggestion from the list or type a correction in the **Change to box**. Click **Change** to change the word to the selected suggestion. (Alternatively, you can click **Change All** to change all occurrences of the misspelled word to the suggestion, click **Ignore** to leave the word alone, or click **Ignore All** to leave all occurrences of the word with its original spelling.)

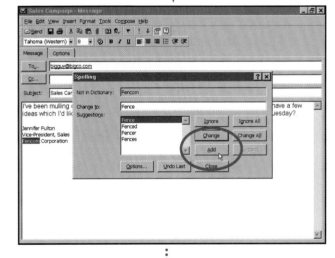

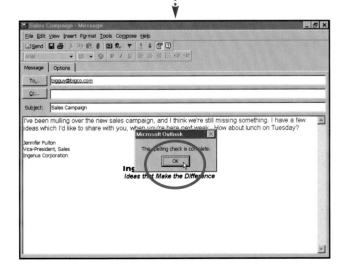

3 Even if you spell a word correctly, if it is not in Outlook's dictionary, the spelling checker flags it. If you use the word frequently (your company name, for example), click the **Add** button to add it to the dictionary so the spell-checking utility will not flag it as a misspelled word.

4 When the spell-checking utility is through, you'll see a message telling you so. Click **OK** to return to your message. ■

Recalling and Resending a Message

"Why would I do this?"

After sending a message, you may remember some bit of information you forgot to add, and you may wish to be able to recall that message and start over. Well, the good news is, you can!

There is a catch, however: You can only recall a message from someone who is logged onto his messaging service, and is using Outlook. Also, if the recipient has already read the message or moved it, then you will not be able to recall it. Once you have recalled the message, you can replace it with a different message. You can, however, resend any message without recalling it first.

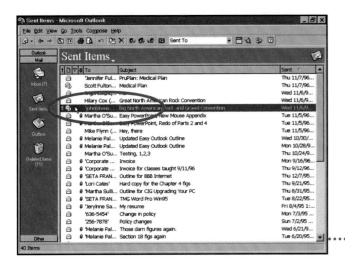

1 If needed, click the **Mail** button on the Outlook bar. Then click **Sent Items**. The contents of the Sent Items folder are displayed. Double-click the message you want to recall. The contents of the message are displayed.

2 Open the **Tools** menu and select **Recall This Message**.

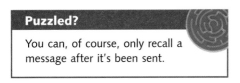

Puzzled?

You can, of course, only recall a message after it's been sent.

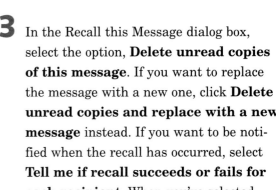

3 In the Recall this Message dialog box, select the option, **Delete unread copies of this message**. If you want to replace the message with a new one, click **Delete unread copies and replace with a new message** instead. If you want to be notified when the recall has occurred, select **Tell me if recall succeeds or fails for each recipient**. When you've selected your option, click **OK**.

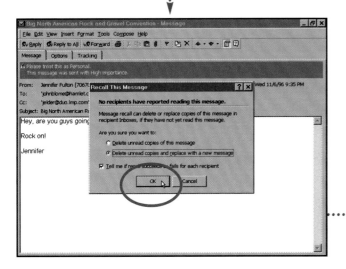

4 If you opted to replace the message with a new one, then the new message window appears. Type the new message and click **Send**.

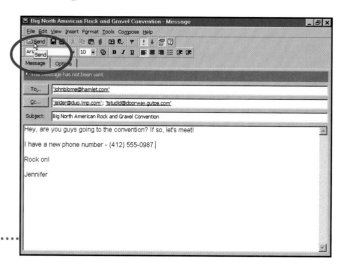

Puzzled?

The new message will only be sent if the old message was successfully recalled.

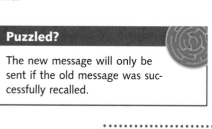

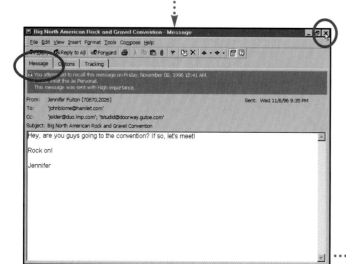

5 You're returned to your original message. A note at the top of the window tells you that you have attempted to recall this message. Click the **Close** button to return to the Sent folder.

Missing Link

This note is helpful if you open a message later on, and you're not sure whether or not you've tried to recall it.

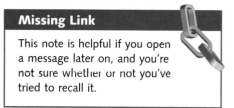

6 To resend a message (rather than recalling and replacing it), switch to the **Sent** folder and open the message by double-clicking it.

Missing Link

You might resend a message that was lost, or accidentally deleted.

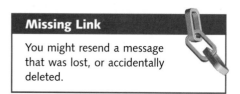

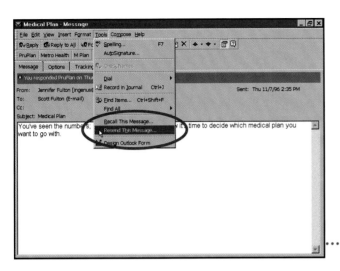

7 Open the **Tools** menu and select **Resend This Message**.

8 A new message window appears, displaying the contents of the original message. Click **Send** to send it.

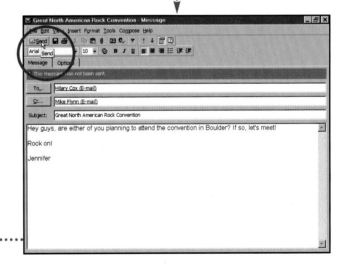

Missing Link

The message at the top of the window reminds you that this copy of your original message has not yet been sent.

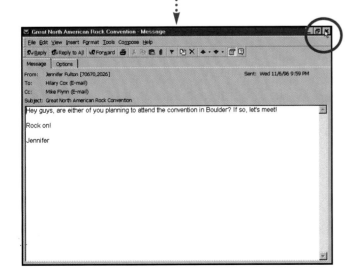

9 The original message window appears. Click its **Close** button to return to the Sent folder. ■

Specifying Where Replies Are Sent

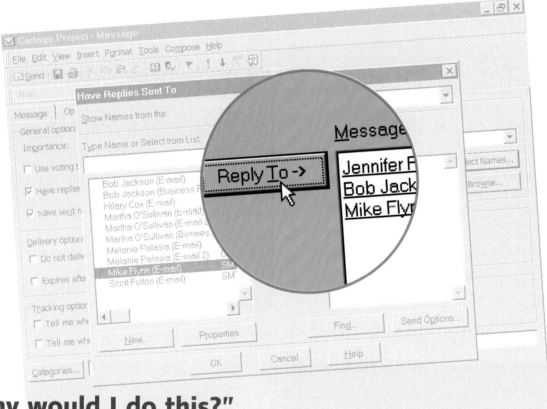

"Why would I do this?"

Normally, if someone opens a message from you and then replies to it, the reply is automatically addressed to you. In some cases, you may wish a subordinate to receive the replies to a particular message instead. For example, if

you've reassigned a project to someone else, you might want him or her to receive the replies to your project queries.

You can also have a copy of the reply sent to you as well as an additional person or persons.

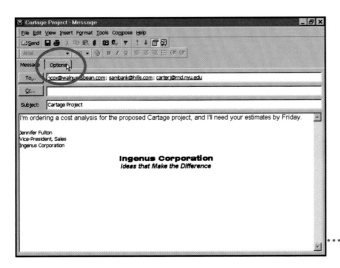

1 After typing the text for your message, click the **Options** tab.

Puzzled?

If you don't want to receive replies to this message at all, then select your name and press **Delete** to remove it.

2 Click the **Have replies sent to** option. Your name automatically appears in the text box. Click the **Select Names** button.

3 Change to the address book that contains the name of the person to whom you want replies sent, by selecting it from the **Show Names from the** list. Click a name in the left-hand list to select it, then click **Reply To**. The name will be listed in the Message Recipients list. Click **OK** to return to the Options tab.

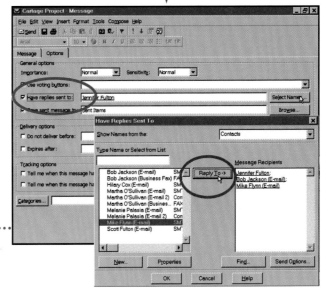

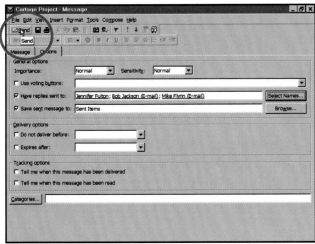

Missing Link

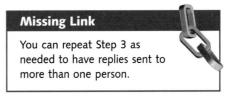

You can repeat Step 3 as needed to have replies sent to more than one person.

4 Click **Send**. Replies to your message will automatically be sent to the people listed in the **Have replies sent to** text box. ■

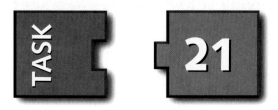

TASK **21**

Checking for Messages

"Why would I do this?"

People may send you e-mail messages frequently, but you'll never know it if you don't, at some time, connect to your messaging service and download (receive) your mail.

You can check for messages on all your services, or just one or two. When you

check for messages, if you have messages in the outbox, they are automatically sent. In addition, with the Rules Wizard update to Outlook installed, you can set up rules for processing messages as they are received. See "Installing Outlook" in the Reference section for help.

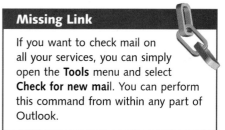

1 If needed, click the **Inbox** icon. Incoming mail is displayed. Open the **Tools** menu and select **Check for new mail on**.

Missing Link

If you want to check mail on all your services, you can simply open the **Tools** menu and select **Check for new mail**. You can perform this command from within any part of Outlook.

2 Select the services you wish to check. Click **OK**, and you're connected to your service. You'll see an animated dialog box depicting the sending and receiving process. After sending and receiving mail from the first service, Outlook automatically disconnects, then connects to the next service you selected.

Missing Link

To Outlook to automatically check for mail, see the options under the service you set up.

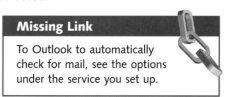

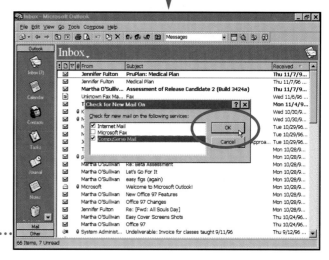

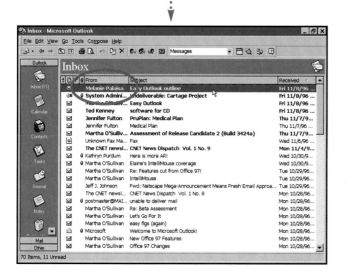

3 After messages are received, they appear in the Inbox. Since messages are sorted by the date they were received, new messages appear at the top of the window. Unread messages are highlighted in bold text. Messages that were not sent are highlighted with a postal icon. ■

Missing Link

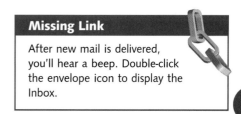

After new mail is delivered, you'll hear a beep. Double-click the envelope icon to display the Inbox.

Checking for Messages Remotely

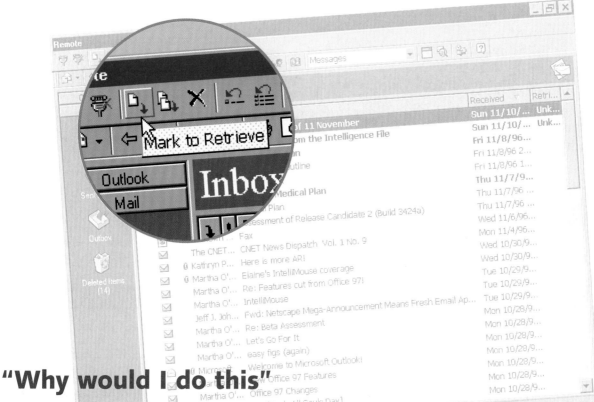

"Why would I do this"

If you're often out of the office on business, there's no reason why you can't still receive your e-mail messages. With remote e-mail, you can dial up your messaging service, obtain a listing of your messages, mark the ones you want to receive right now, then download (receive) the messages you marked.

You can use remote mail even if you're not out of the office; for example, if you want to "preview" your mail when you're busy and only download the messages you need right now.

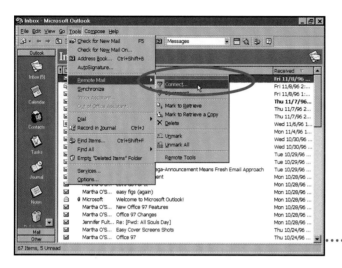

1 If needed, click the **Inbox** icon. Incoming mail is displayed. Open the **Tools** menu and select **Remote Mail**, then select **Connect**.

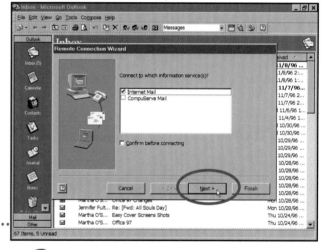

2 In the Remote Connection Wizard, select the messaging service(s) you want to check by clicking them. Then click **Next>**.

3 If you have any outgoing messages, you can send them now. If you don't want to send a particular item, click it to deselect it. Then click **Finish**. You're connected to each service in turn.

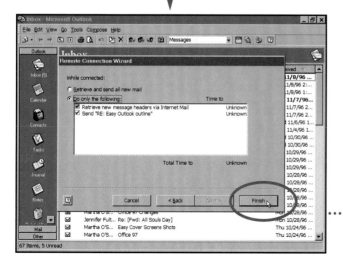

Missing Link

If you want to simply send and receive all your mail without looking at your message headers, then click the **Retrieve and send all new mail** option.

Task 22: Checking for Messages Remotely

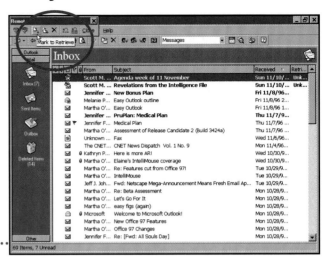

4 Click the **Inbox** icon in the Outlook bar. New messages appear in the Inbox list, marked with a remote icon (an envelope with a small telephone). Click the **Mark to Retrieve** button on the Remote toolbar. Then click the messages you want to retrieve.

5 Click the **Connect** button on the Remote toolbar.

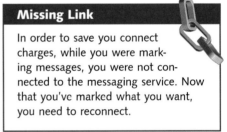

Missing Link

In order to save you connect charges, while you were marking messages, you were not connected to the messaging service. Now that you've marked what you want, you need to reconnect.

6 The Remote Connection Wizard displays. The messaging service you marked earlier should still be marked, so simply click **Next**.

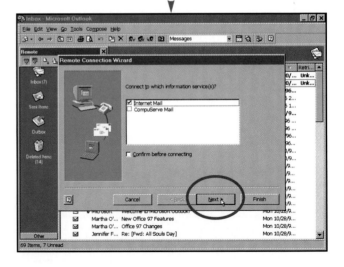

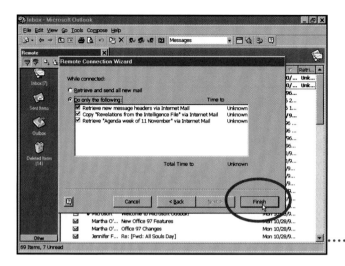

7 Verify that you've marked the right messages to retrieve, then click **Finish**. You're connected to the service you selected, and the messages you marked are retrieved.

8 Click the **Close Preview** button on the Remote toolbar to remove it from the screen. ■

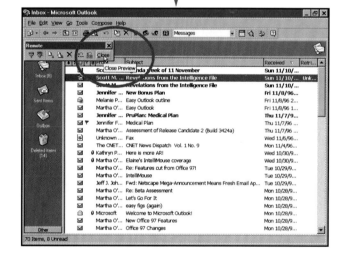

Reading a Message

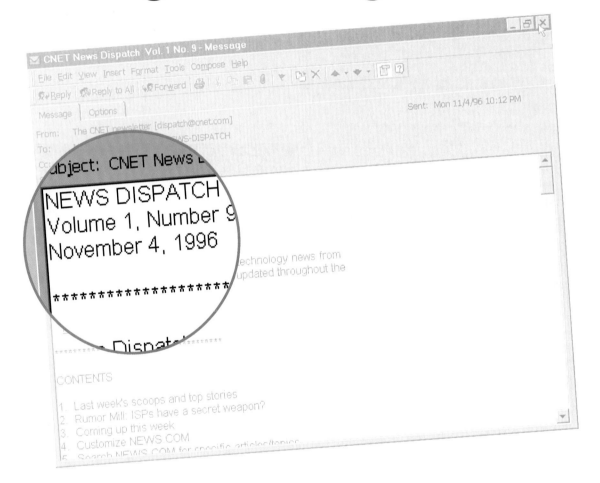

"Why would I do this?"

In order to view the contents of a message, you must open it to read it. Opening a message is as simple as double-clicking, as you'll soon learn.

Once you've read a message, you can reply to it, forward it, file it, or print it. Also, after reading the message, you can delete it from your system.

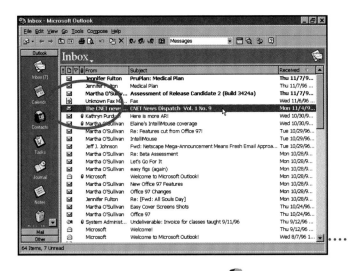

1 Incoming messages are stored in the Inbox, so click the **Inbox** icon on the Outlook bar. A list of incoming messages is displayed. Unread messages appear in bold text. To open a message so you can read it, double-click the message header. The message window opens.

Missing Link

You can sort your messages however you like. To sort them by the sender for example, click the **From** button at the top of the Inbox window.

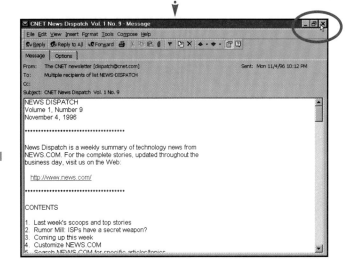

2 After reading the message, click its **Close** button, and you're returned to the Inbox. ■

Missing Link

If you download the 3-pane extension update for Outlook from Microsoft's Web Site, you can preview the contents of a message by simply clicking it in Step 1. See "Installing Outlook" in the Reference section for help.

Flagging Messages

"Why would I do this?"

You can flag messages which are important to you. For example, if a particular message requires a follow-up, or if it contains important information you don't want to forget, you can flag it.

You can add flags (such as "Review," or "Call") to messages you're sending. The flag appears at the top of the message window.

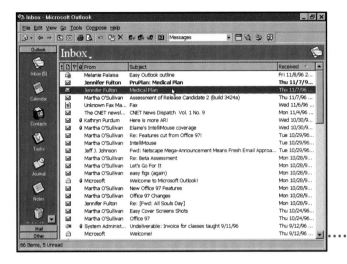

1 Open the message you want to flag by double-clicking it.

Puzzled?

If you want to flag a message you're sending, type the text of the message first, then proceed to Step 2.

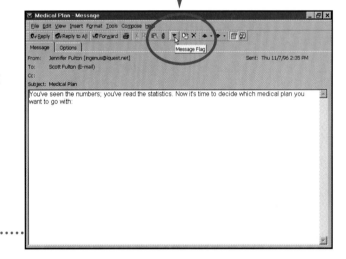

2 Click the **Flag Message** button. The Flag Message dialog box appears.

Missing Link

The flag will appear above the text in the message window.

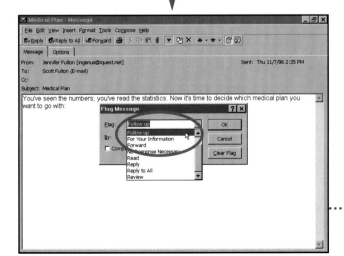

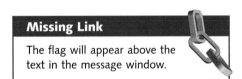

3 Select a flag from the **Flag** list.

Puzzled?

If you don't see a flag you like, type your own in the text box.

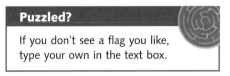

4 You can set a due date for the flag by selecting from the **By** list. When you open the list, the current month is shown. To move to the next month, click the right arrow at the top of the calendar. Click **OK**, and you're returned to the message window.

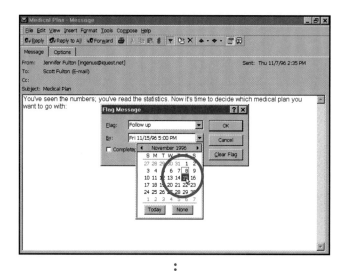

Missing Link

You can reopen this message. Click the **Flag Message** button, and use this dialog box to mark the flag as **Completed**. You can also use the **Clear Flag** button.

5 The flag you selected appears at the top of the message window. Click the **Close** button to return to the Inbox.

6 A flag appears in front of the message in the Inbox window. ■

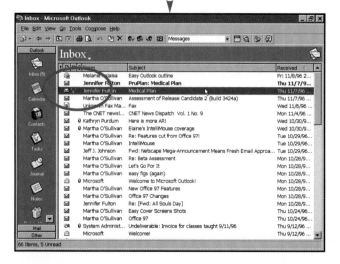

Saving an Attached File

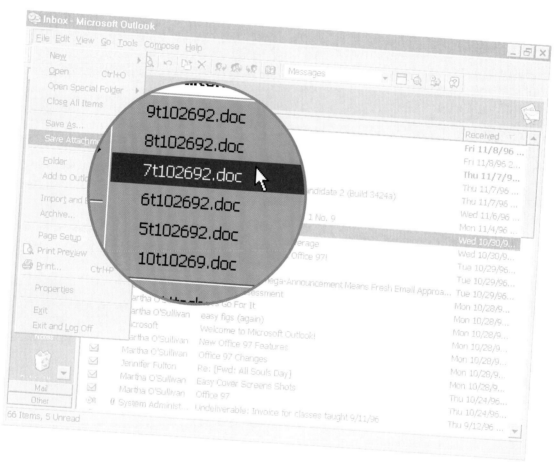

"Why would I do this?"

If someone has attached a file to one of your messages, you might want to save it to your hard disk before you open the file or make any changes to it.

Although you can open an attached file (and even make changes to it) *without saving the file to your hard disk first*, if you don't save the file to your hard disk at some point, your changes will be lost.

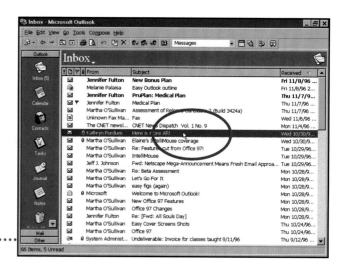

1 Messages which contain attached files appear with a paper clip icon. To save the attached file(s) to your hard disk, click the message to select it.

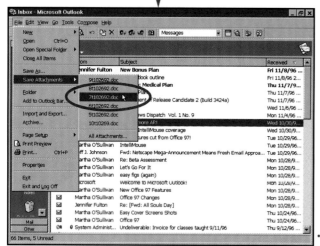

2 Open the **File** menu and select **Save Attachments**. A menu listing the attached files appears. Select the file you wish to save, or select **All attachments**.

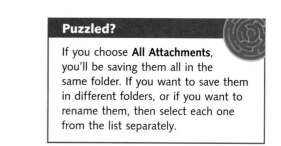

Puzzled?

If you choose **All Attachments**, you'll be saving them all in the same folder. If you want to save them in different folders, or if you want to rename them, then select each one from the list separately.

3 Select the folder in which you want to save the file. To change to a different file or drive, select it from the **Save in** list. When you're ready to save the file to your hard disk, click **Save**. You're returned to the Inbox. ■

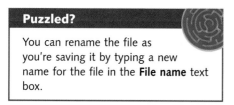

Puzzled?

You can rename the file as you're saving it by typing a new name for the file in the **File name** text box.

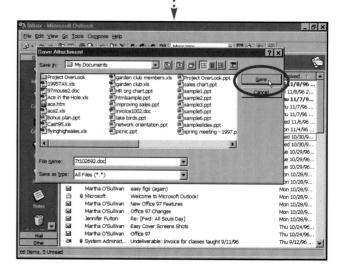

Replying to a Message

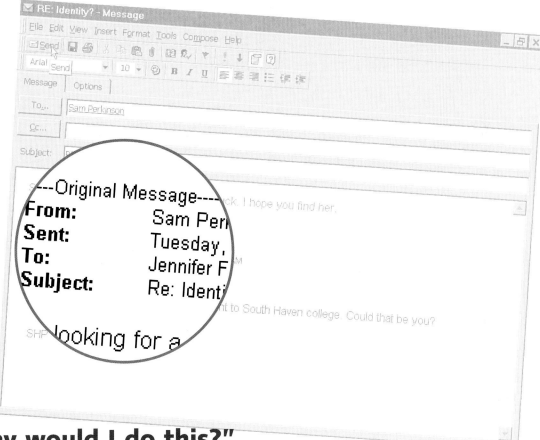

"Why would I do this?"

Sometimes, in a message, a person may ask you a question, or issue a statement to which you feel you must reply. When you reply to a message, the contents of the original message are copied to your reply. This helps the recipient remember exactly the words to which you are referring.

You can send your reply to just the originator, or to the originator and all the recipients of the original message.

1 If needed, click the **Inbox** icon. Incoming messages are displayed. Select the message to which you want to reply by clicking it.

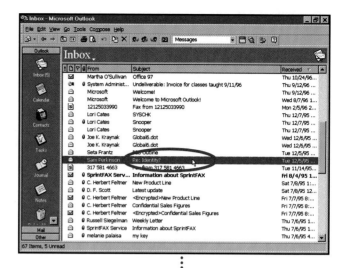

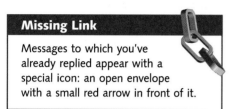

Missing Link

Messages to which you've already replied appear with a special icon: an open envelope with a small red arrow in front of it.

2 To send your reply to the originator only, click the **Reply** button on the Standard toolbar. To send your reply to all of the recipients of the original message, click the **Reply to All** button instead (it's located to the right of the Reply button).

3 The text of the original message appears in the message window. Type your reply above this text, then click **Send**.

Puzzled?

You can delete the text of the original message if you like. Just drag over the text to select it, then press **Delete** to remove it.

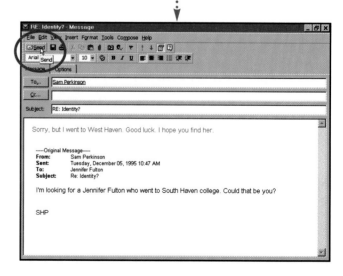

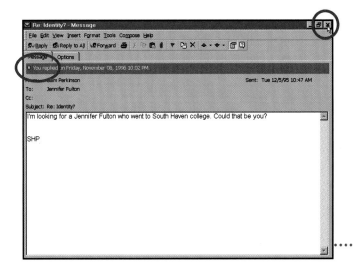

4 You're returned to the original message window. A notice appears above the text, reminding you (should you open this message again), that you've already replied to this message. Click its **Close** button to return to Inbox.

5 The Replied to icon appears in front of the message in the Inbox window. It looks like an open envelope, with a small red arrow in front of it. ■

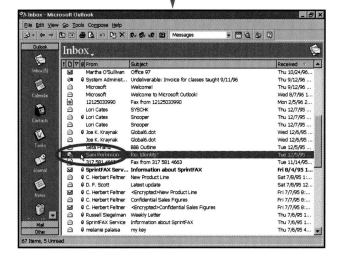

85

Forwarding a Message

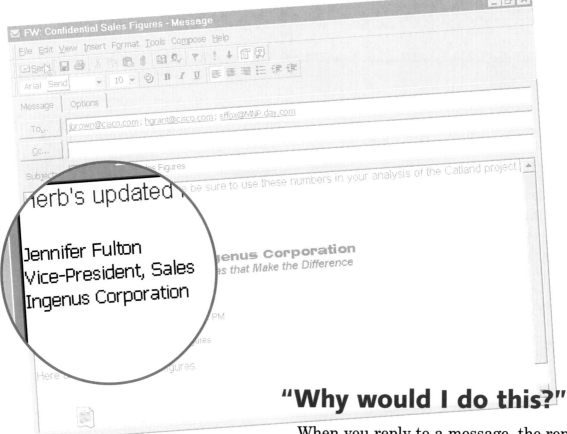

"Why would I do this?"

When you reply to a message, the reply is automatically addressed to the sender of the original message. When you forward a message instead, you can send it to anyone you want.

You might forward a message if it was sent to the wrong person, if the project to which it refers has been reassigned to someone else, or if you know of someone who should be made aware of its information.

1 If needed, click the **Inbox** icon. Incoming messages are displayed. Select the message you want to forward by clicking it. Click **Forward**.

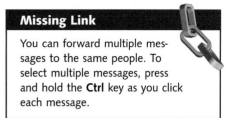

Missing Link

You can forward multiple messages to the same people. To select multiple messages, press and hold the **Ctrl** key as you click each message.

2 A new message window appears. The text of the original message appears at the bottom of the text box. If you want to add a comment to the forwarded message, type it above this text.

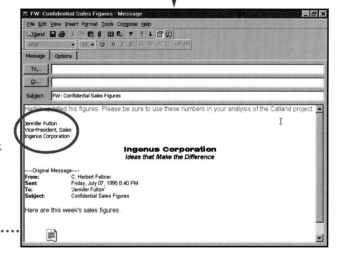

3 In the **To** text box, type the address of the person to whom you wish to send your message, or click the **To** button to select one from your address book. You can send a copy of the message to someone by including their address in the **Cc** box. If you're forwarding multiple messages, then type a **Subject** too. When you're ready, click **Send**. The message appears in the Inbox with the Forward icon, an open envelope with a small blue arrow. ■

Printing a Message

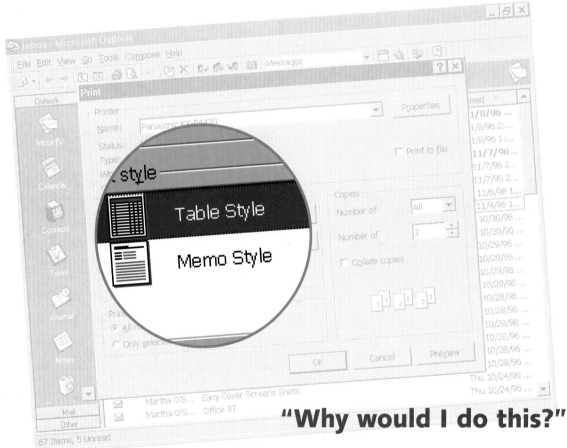

"Why would I do this?"

You might want to print a message in order to take it with you to a meeting, or an out-of-town conference. You might also want to print out a copy of a message for your files.

You can change the paper size, change the orientation, and add a header or footer. In order to see if you'll like your changes, you can preview them before you print.

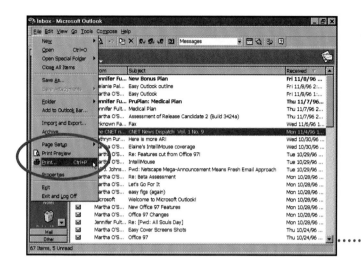

1 If needed, click the Inbox icon. Incoming messages are displayed. Select the message you want to print by clicking it. If you want to print several messages at once, press and hold the **Ctrl** key as you click each one. (If you want to print all the messages in a long list, use the instructions in Step 2.) Then open the **File** menu and select **Print**. Then continue with Step 3.

2 To print the selected messages in a long list, select **Table Style**. When you select this option, you can elect to print the entire message list, or only selected messages. Click the option you want in the **Print range** area. Click **Page Setup,** then skip to Step 4.

Puzzled?

If you click the **Print** button, your message will print with the default settings. You will not be able to make any adjustments.

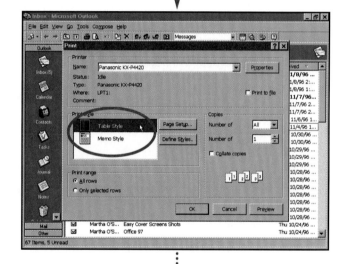

3 To print the contents of each message, select **Memo style**. When you choose this option, you can elect to print each message on a new page, or to print the contents of any attached files. Select the options you want from the **Print options** area. Then click **Page Setup**.

4 With the options on the **Format** tab, you can change the text font used in printing the messages. For example, to change the title font, click the **Font** button in the **Title** area, select a font, and click **OK**. Click the **Paper** tab.

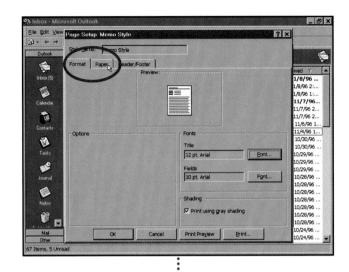

Puzzled?

If you're going to be faxing the print, or if you have a color printer, you may wish to deselect the **Print using gray shading** option.

5 On the Paper tab, choose paper size from the **Paper Type** list. Select a layout from the **Page Size** list. Adjust the **Margins** and the **Orientation** if you like. Click the **Header/Footer** tab.

Missing Link

Orientation refers to the direction the text prints on the page. In Portrait, text prints across the shortest width of the paper. In Landscape, text prints along the paper's largest width.

6 To create a header or a footer, enter what you want in the appropriate text box. For example, notice the page number is already set to print in the middle of the footer. To insert text, click the text box and type. Insert additional information with the buttons located under the footer area. Click the first button to insert the page number, the second to insert the total number of pages, the third to insert the date, the fourth to insert the time, and the last button to insert your name. Click **Print Preview**.

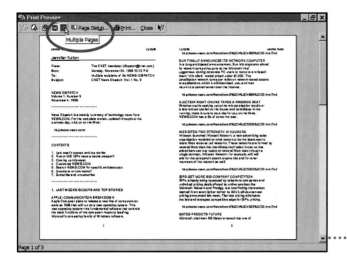

7 Here you can see what your printout will look like before you actually print it. If something's wrong, you can return to the Page Setup dialog box by clicking **Page Setup**. To see several pages at once, click the **Multiple Pages** button.

8 When you're ready to print, click **Print**, and you're returned to the Print dialog box.

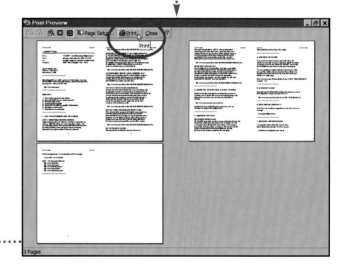

Missing Link

You can follow these same basic steps to print any Outlook item.

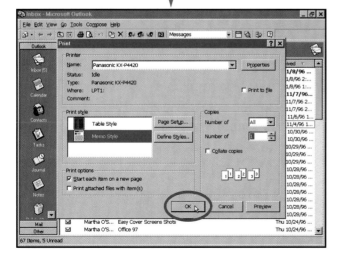

9 Click **OK** to print your message(s). ■

TASK

29

Sending and Receiving a Fax

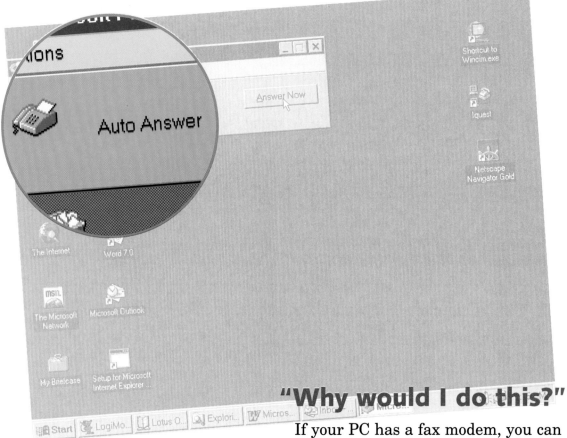

"Why would I do this?"

If your PC has a fax modem, you can send a fax directly from your computer. You can also receive faxes directly. The most obvious reason for using Outlook to coordinate your faxes is the convenience: no more trips to the fax machine, no more waiting in line, and no more lost faxes.

In order to use this feature, you must have the fax service installed. See Task 9 for help.

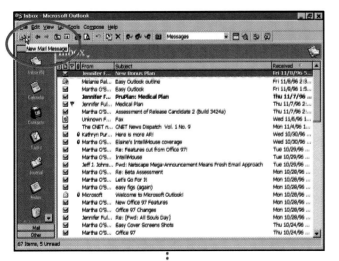

1 To send a fax, you follow the same basic steps that you do to create an e-mail message: From within Inbox, click the **New Mail Message** button.

Missing Link

You can jazz up your fax by choosing one of the message templates: Open the **File** menu, select **New**, then select **Choose Template**. Select a template and click **OK**.

2 Click the **To** button. The Select Names dialog box appears.

3 If needed, switch to the Contact list by selecting it from the **Show Names from the** list. Select a contact's fax number from the list on the left and click **To**. Click **OK**.

Puzzled?

You can send the same fax to multiple people by repeating Step 3 as needed.

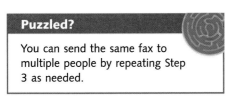

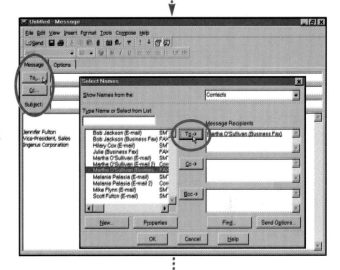

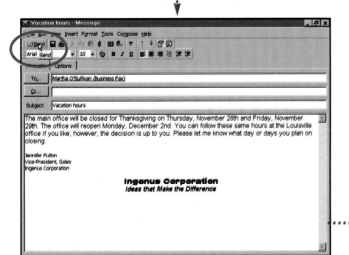

4 Type a **Subject**. Enter your message in the text box at the bottom of the window. To send the fax, click **Send**. Microsoft Fax prepares the text of your fax for sending. It then dials the number and sends your fax.

5 To set up your system to receive a fax, open the **Tools** menu and select **Check for new mail on**.

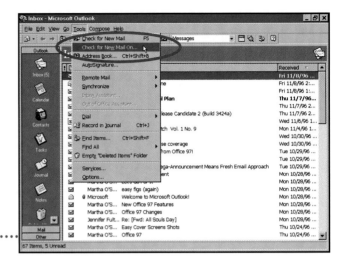

Puzzled?

If the Microsoft Fax program is not listed, you'll need to install it as a service under Outlook. See Task 9 for help.

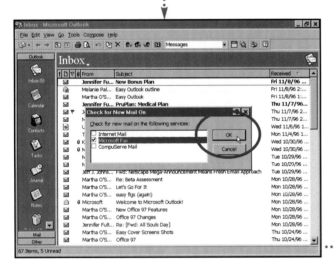

6 Select the **Microsoft Fax** program and click **OK**.

Puzzled?

If Microsoft Fax is not set up to answer automatically, you can trigger it by clicking **Answer Now**. To change it so it will answer automatically, open the **Options** menu, select **Modem Properties**, then set the **Answer after XX rings** option to something small such as 3 rings, and click **OK**.

7 Microsoft Fax opens its window and waits. When a fax machine dials your modem, Microsoft Fax will automatically answer and receive the fax. (Microsoft Fax stays active—and ready to receive additional faxes) as long as Outlook is still running. New faxes appear in your Inbox. ■

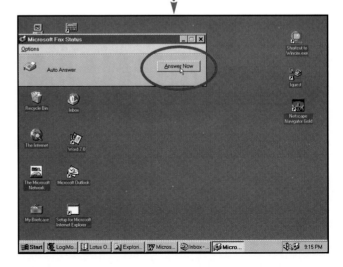

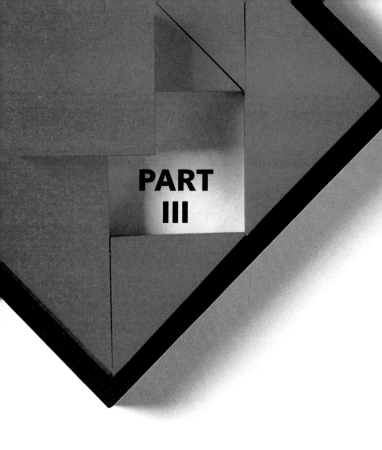

PART III

Tracking Events with Calendar

YOU CAN KEEP TRACK OF all the important events in your life (meetings, appointments, anniversaries, birthdays, and holidays) with the Calendar. If you're like most people, keeping track of events such as these help you to avoid missing something important.

In Outlook, an *appointment* is an event which you schedule time for, but which does not involve inviting other people in the company. A *meeting,* on the other hand, involves sending and receiving meeting requests and scheduling meeting resources such as a room or A/V equipment and so on. An *event* is an activity which lasts a day or more, such as your vacation, a convention, a trade show, a birthday, anniversary, or special holiday.

When you schedule an appointment or meeting, you can use real words such as next Monday or noon. Outlook understands what you mean and translates it into a real date such as November 11, and a real time such as 12:00 PM. If you want to be reminded a few minutes before your upcoming appointment or meeting, you can set Outlook to beep you ahead of time.

You can mark appointments as busy, free, tentative, or out of office. In addition, you can grant others permission to schedule appointments for you and to make changes to them.

Outlook also lets you schedule recurring appointments and meetings such as weekly or monthly meetings, workouts, doctor's appointments, and salon visits. In addition, you can easily move appointments and meetings when needed.

If you have to schedule a lot of meetings, you'll find the Meeting Planner very helpful. With it, you can send out meeting requests, schedule a meeting room, along with any equipment you might need, such as a slide or overhead projector. Best of all, the AutoPick feature makes it easy to determine the best time for everyone to meet. As your coworkers respond to your meeting requests, their responses appear as simple e-mail messages in your Inbox. You can track the results of your requests through the Meeting Planner in the Calendar.

Outlook supports two types of events: singular and annual. A singular event might last for a day or even several days. For example, you might want to schedule a convention, your vacation, a training class or seminar, and other singular events. Typical annual events include such things as anniversaries, birthdays, and special holidays. When you schedule an event, it appears as a banner heading at the top of the day(s) in which it occurs—this is different from an appointment or a meeting, which appears within the time segments of a particular day.

Adding holidays to a new calendar can often be difficult, however, Outlook makes it easy. You can import a listing of common holidays into your Calendar with a few mouse clicks. Holidays are sorted by country, so if you travel often, you can add the common holidays for the countries to which you travel to your Calendar as well.

After entering your various appointments, meetings, and events, you can print them out and take them with you when you're out of the office. You can print a day' worth of appointments on a single page, or a week, or a month. You can print notes and tasks with your Calendar as well. Outlook supports several page styles, enabling you to insert your printouts into your paper day planner, including popular day planners such as Day Runner, Day Timer, and Franklin Day Planner.

Moving Around the Calendar

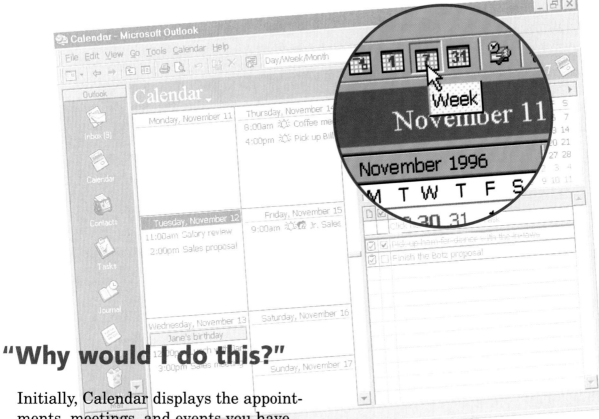

"Why would I do this?"

Initially, Calendar displays the appointments, meetings, and events you have set up for today. To view appointments for another day, you'll need to change from one day to another in Calendar.

Also, if you need to, you can view several days worth of appointments at one time, or even a whole month's worth!

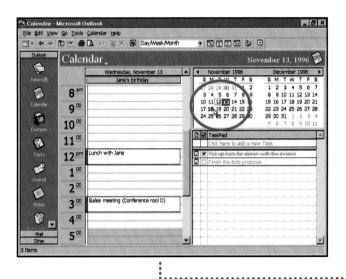

1 In the upper right corner of the Calendar window, you'll find the Date Navigator. With it, you can easily move from one date to the next. The current date appears in blue. Today's date is marked by a red outline. To move to a day that is visible in the Date Navigator, click that date.

Missing Link

You can view several days at once by pressing **Ctrl** and clicking the days you want to view.

2 The Calendar is displayed on the left. To move to a month that is not visible, click one of the month labels (such as November or December) and choose the month you want from the list which appears. For example, click November and select January.

Puzzled?

You can also move from month to month by clicking the left or right arrows on the Date Navigator.

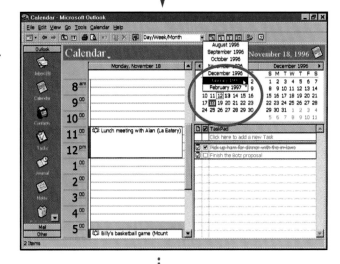

3 The Calendar for January is displayed on the left. To view a week or a month's worth of appointments click the appropriate **View** button, such as the **Week** button, or the month. To view today's appointments, click the **Go to Today** button on the Standard toolbar. ■

Missing Link

If a date appears in bold within the Date Navigator, then you have an appointment, meeting, or event scheduled for that day.

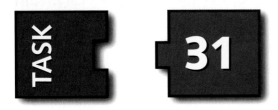

Scheduling an Appointment

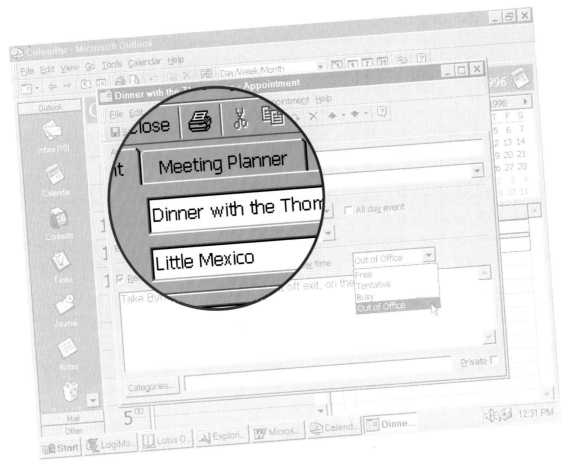

"Why would I do this?"

An *appointment* is personal; it does not involve company personnel or resources, as a meeting might. You can schedule an appointment for any type of activity, such as a doctor's appointment, a lunch date, your workout, or a client meeting.

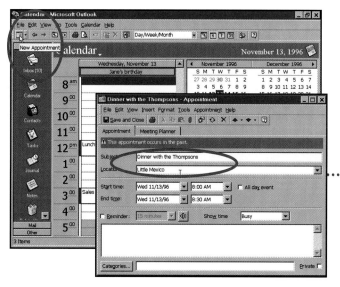

1 Click the **New Appointment** button on the Standard toolbar.

2 Type a description of the appointment in the **Subject** text box. Enter the location of the appointment in the **Location** text box.

Missing Link

Change to the day on which you want the appointment to appear, prior to clicking the **New Appointment** button. In addition, you can click the start time prior to clicking **New Appointment**.

3 Enter a start date and time. To select a start date, click the down arrow on the **Start time** list to display the calendar. Then click a date. To change to a different month, click the left or right arrows at the top of the calendar window. To select a time, click the down arrow on the time list and scroll to select the time you want. Enter an end date and time. If you want to block out the entire day, click **All day event**.

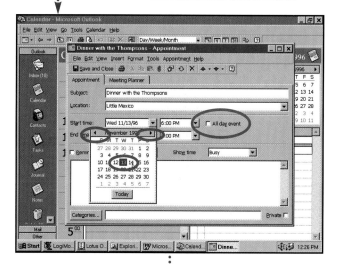

4 If you want to be reminded of your appointment prior to its start time, click **Reminder**. Click the down arrow and select the number of minutes prior to the appointment at which you want the reminder to go off.

Missing Link

Change the sound that is played during the reminder by clicking the horn button.

5 Select how you want your appointment to appear to those who have access to your calendar by selecting an option from the **Show time** list. You can also add a note, such as directions or things to bring, and so on in the large text box.

Puzzled?

If you don't want anyone to have access to the details of this appointment, click **Private** in the lower-right corner of the Event box.

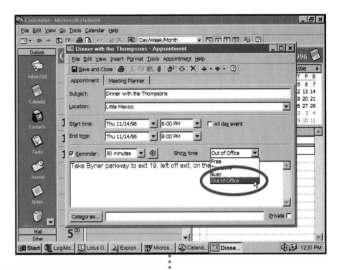

6 Click the **Categories** button to select a category for this appointment. You can later search and sort your appointments by this category.

7 Select the categories you want to assign to this appointment and click **OK**.

8 You're returned to the New Appointment dialog box. When you're through selecting options, click **Save and Close**. You're new appointment appears in the Calendar. ■

Missing Link

Create a new appointment by dragging e-mail message from the Inbox to the Calendar icon on the Outlook bar. The subject of the message becomes the subject of your appointment, and the text appears in the New Appointment dialog box.

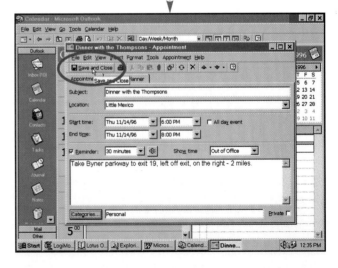

Scheduling a Meeting

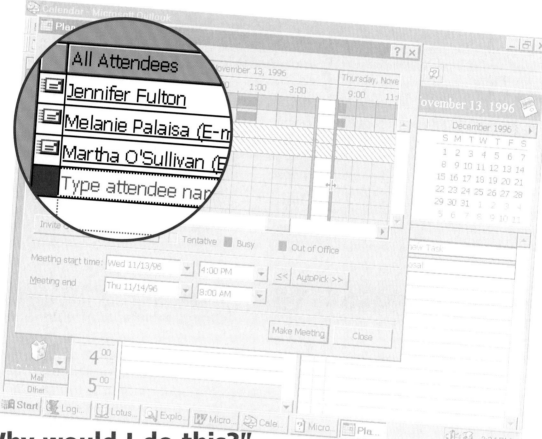

"Why would I do this?"

A meeting is an appointment which involves other company personnel. When you schedule a meeting, e-mail requests are sent out over your company's network, inviting the people you selected to attend. When they respond to your request, their individual responses appear as e-mail messages in your Inbox. However, you can access a summary of those responses through the Meeting Planner in the Calendar.

When scheduling a meeting, you can also reserve the other resources you might need, such as a particular meeting room, a projector, and other equipment.

Task 32: Scheduling a Meeting

1 In the Calendar, change to the day on which you want to add the meeting. Then double-click the meeting's start time, or click the **Plan a Meeting** button on the Standard toolbar.

Puzzled?

In Outlook, you can schedule a meeting with any of your coworkers, provided that you are all connected to a company network. If you're not on a network, you can still use the meeting planner; however, meeting responses are not automatically tabulated.

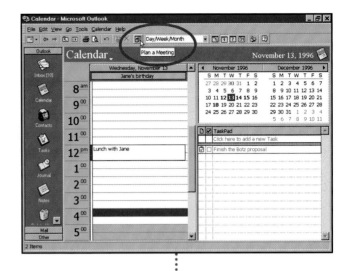

2 Click **Invite Others**.

Missing Link

You can create a meeting quickly by dragging an e-mail message from the Inbox to the Calendar icon on the Outlook bar. A message window will appear; simply click the **Meeting Planner** tab to begin.

3 The Select Attendees and Resources dialog box appears. Select the address book you want to use from the **Show Names from the** list. Select a name by clicking it. Then click either the **Required** button or the **Optional** button (for people whose presence is optional or required). Click **OK**.

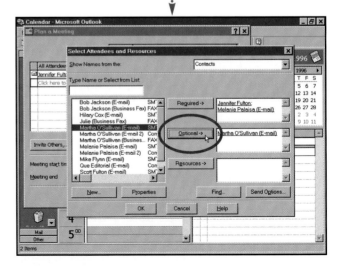

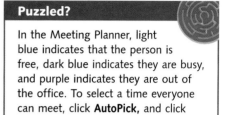

4 Select a start and end time from the **Meeting start time** and **Meeting end** lists. Click **Make Meeting**.

> ### Puzzled?
>
> In the Meeting Planner, light blue indicates that the person is free, dark blue indicates they are busy, and purple indicates they are out of the office. To select a time everyone can meet, click **AutoPick,** and click **Make Meeting**.

5 An e-mail message window appears. Enter a **Subject**, **Location**, and a text message. You can also select a category for the message, and attach a file (such as the agenda) to the message. When you're ready, click **Send**.

> ### Puzzled?
>
> If you change your mind prior to sending the invitations, click **Cancel Invitation**. If you need to cancel a meeting later on, then double-click the meeting block. Open the **Appointment** menu and select **Cancel Meeting**.

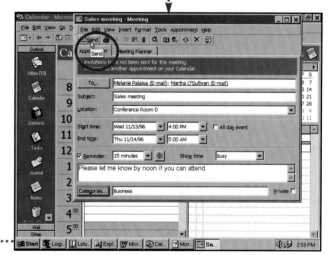

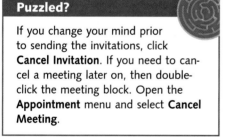

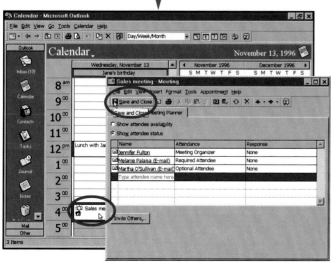

6 The meeting appears in your calendar. After attendees have responded to your meeting request, you can view their responses by double-clicking the meeting (provided the attendees are connected to your company's network).

7 The Meeting window appears. Click the **Meeting Planner** tab. If needed, click **Show attendee status**, and you'll see a listing of each individual's response. Click **Save and Close** to return to Calendar. ■

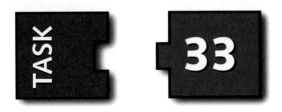

TASK **33**

Scheduling an Event

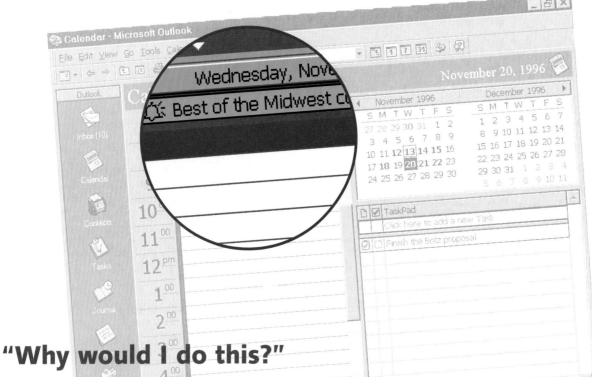

"Why would I do this?"

An *event* is an activity which often takes place over the entire day, or several days. Typical events include birthdays, anniversaries, and holidays. They also include seminars, all-day training sessions, conferences, retreats, and vacations.

When you enter an event into the Calendar, it appears at the top of the day on which it occurs. Individual time slots are not blocked out; the reasoning here is that often, an event (such as a birthday) does not prevent you from attending other meetings or appointments.

1 Switch to the date on which you want the event to occur, then open the **Calendar** menu and select **New Event**.

Missing Link

To create an event quickly, double-click the date heading for the day on which the event will occur. You can also drag an e-mail message from the Inbox to the Calendar to create an event. A message window appears. Continue with Step 2.

2 Type a name or description for the event in the **Subject** box. If there's a location associated with the event, enter it in the **Location** box. If the event occurs over several days, select an **End date** for the event. Also, if you like, you can add a note in the large text box.

Missing Link

Normally, the time allotted to an event is shown as Free in your Calendar. You might want to change it to Out of office by selecting that option from the **Show time** list.

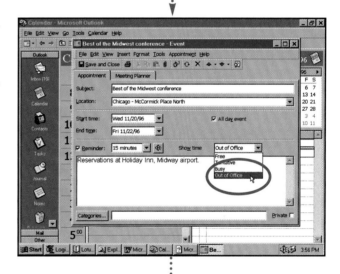

3 When you're through, click **Save and Close**. The name of the event appears as a heading above the time slots for the date(s) you indicated. ■

Puzzled?

A particular day can contain more than one event; for example, you might be attending a conference the same day as someone's birthday. In that case, both events will appear at the top of that day's calendar.

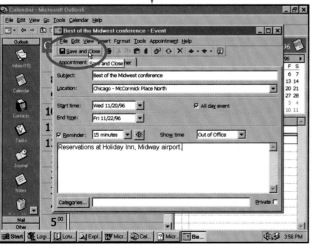

Scheduling a Recurring Appointment, Meeting, or Event

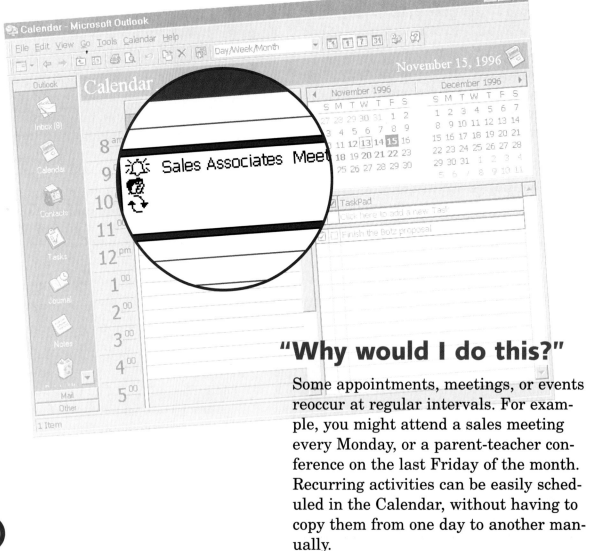

"Why would I do this?"

Some appointments, meetings, or events reoccur at regular intervals. For example, you might attend a sales meeting every Monday, or a parent-teacher conference on the last Friday of the month. Recurring activities can be easily scheduled in the Calendar, without having to copy them from one day to another manually.

Task 34: Scheduling a Recurring Appointment, Meeting, or Event

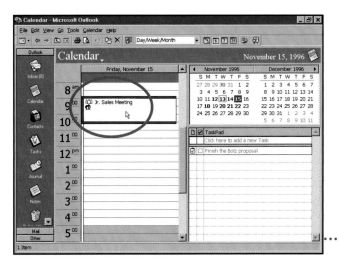

1 If the appointment, meeting, or event which you want to make recurring is not open, then double-click it to open it.

Puzzled?

You can complete these steps when creating a new activity, in order to make it recurring. You can also complete these steps after the fact, if you learn later on that an activity will reoccur.

2 The appointment, meeting, or event window appears. Click the **Recurrence** button. The Recurrence dialog box appears.

3 Select a recurrence pattern, such as **Daily**. When you select Daily, you can enter an interval, such as every other day, by entering a 2 in the Every XX day(s) box. You can also select **Every weekday**, which would make the activity reoccur every Monday through Friday. You can stop the activity after a particular date by selecting that date from the **End by** list. You can also set a limit for the number of times the activity will reoccur.

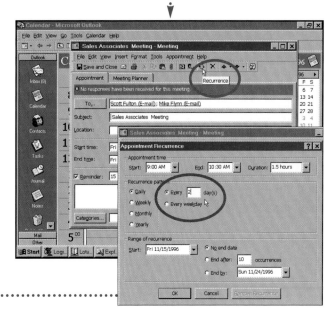

4 If you selected the **Weekly** recurrence pattern, then you can have the activity recur every third week by entering a 3 in the Recur every XX week(s) box. You can also select the day on which the event recurs. In the **Range of recurrence** area, select a stop time for the activity, if any. Click **OK**, and skip to Step 7.

5 If you selected the **Monthly** recurrence pattern, then select whether you want the activity to reoccur on the same date of every month (such as the 15th), or if you want it to reoccur on a particular day of the week, such as every third Friday. In the **Range of recurrence** area, select a stop time for the activity, if any. Click **OK** and skip to Step 7.

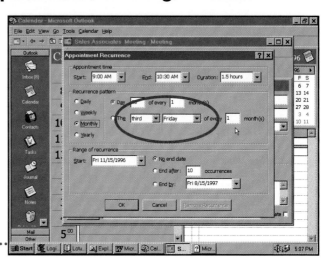

6 If you selected the **Yearly** recurrence pattern, you can select whether the event occurs on the same date each year, or on a particular day of the week within a particular month. In the **Range of recurrence** area, select a stop time for the activity, if any. When you're through selecting options, click **OK**.

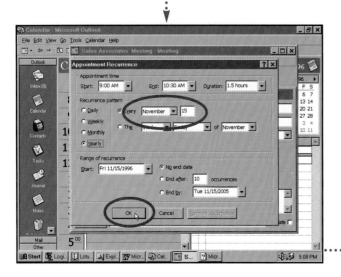

7 You're returned to the appointment, meeting, or event window. Click **Save and Close**. The activity is copied to the Calendar, using the recurring pattern you selected. Recurring activities are marked with a special icon, two bent arrows which form a circle. ■

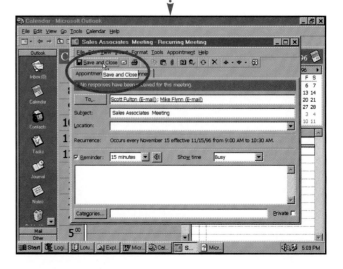

Puzzled?

If you changed a meeting, you'll be asked if you want to send an update to the attendees in the form of an e-mail message. Click **Yes**.

TASK 35

Responding to a Meeting Request

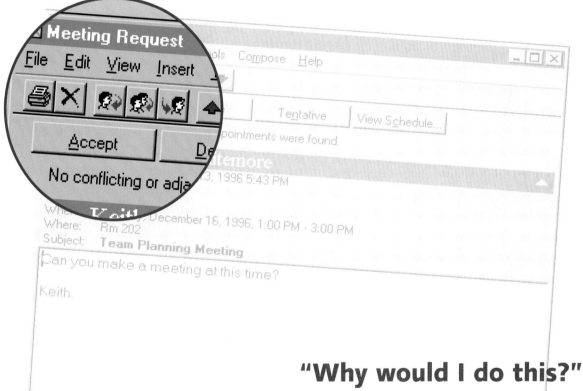

"Why would I do this?"

Obviously, if someone sends you a request for a meeting, you need to respond. When you respond, you can accept the invitation, reject it, or accept it tentatively. When you accept an invitation to attend a meeting, it's automatically added to your Calendar so you won't forget about it.

1 Switch to the Inbox and double-click the meeting request to open it.

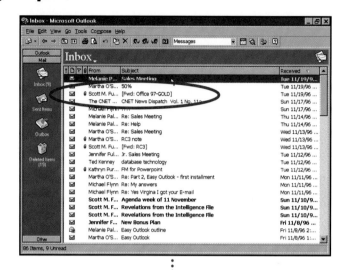

Missing Link

If you're on a company network, you might be able to setup Outlook to automatically respond to meeting requests from coworkers. Open the **Tools** menu, select **Options**, then click the **Calendar** tab. Click **Advanced Scheduling** to select the options you want.

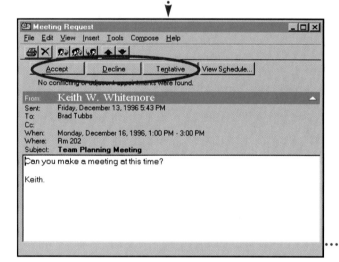

2 You'll find some buttons at the top of the message window. Click either **Accept**, **Tentative**, or **Decline**, depending on how you wish to respond.

Puzzled?

If you want to check your Calendar before you respond to the meeting request, then click **View in Calendar**.

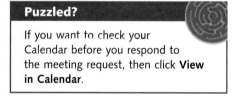

3 Click **Send** to send your response. ■

Missing Link

If you receive a meeting cancellation, click **Remove from Calendar** to remove the meeting from your Calendar. The cancellation notification is also removed from your Inbox.

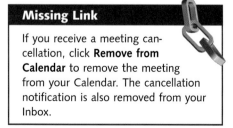

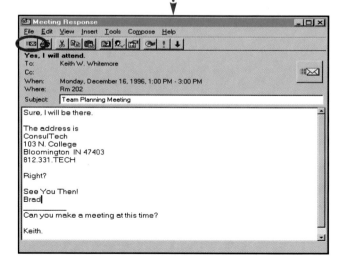

Changing an Appointment, Meeting, or Event

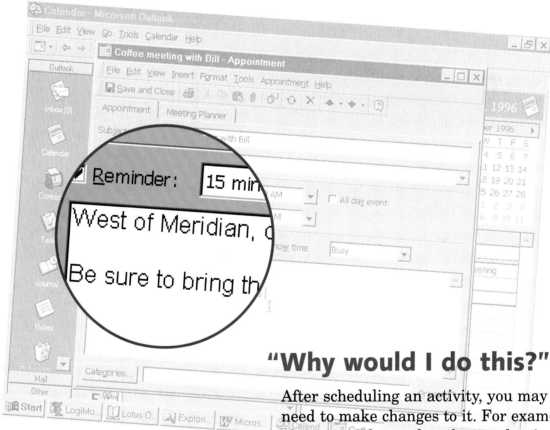

"Why would I do this?"

After scheduling an activity, you may need to make changes to it. For example, you might need to change the time of the activity, or its location.

Changing an appointment, meeting, or event follows a similar pattern: basically, you open the activity, make your changes, and then save them, as you'll learn in this task.

1 First, open the activity you want to change. For example, double-click an appointment within your Calendar.

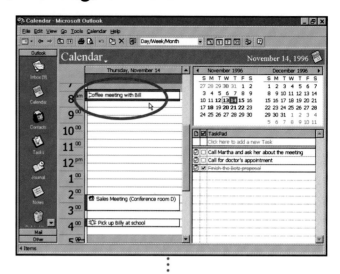

Missing Link

You can move an appointment, meeting, or event, by simply dragging it onto the Date Navigator and dropping it on the date to which you want to move it. You can also move an activity within the day on which it occurs by again dragging and dropping it where you want.

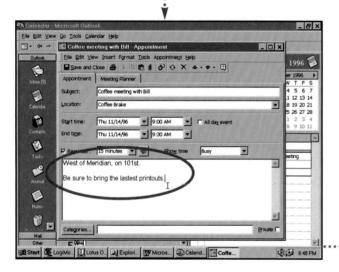

2 The appointment window appears. Make your changes. You can change the time, description, or location of the activity. You can also add a note in the large text box.

Puzzled?

If you change the start time for an activity, the end time is automatically adjusted.

3 Click **Save and Close** to save your changes. ■

Missing Link

If you make changes to a meeting, you'll be asked whether or not you want to send an update (in the form of an e-mail message) to the attendees. Click **Yes**.

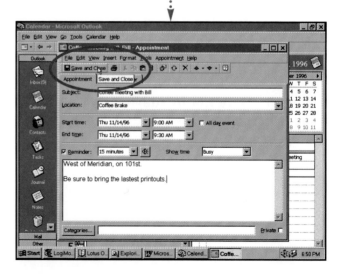

Adding Holidays

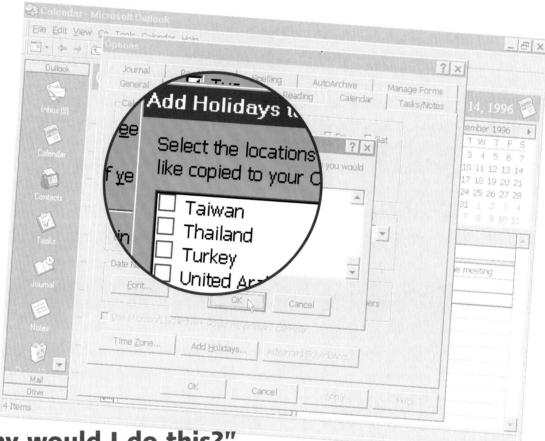

"Why would I do this?"

When you first start using the Calendar, national holidays such as Thanksgiving, and so on, do not automatically appear. You can add holidays yourself, by simply adding an event and making it recurring.

However, that's a lot of trouble. Instead, you can have Outlook automatically update your Calendar with its list of holidays. Holidays are grouped by country, so if you travel a lot, you can add the holidays for more than one country to your Calendar.

Task 37: Adding Holidays

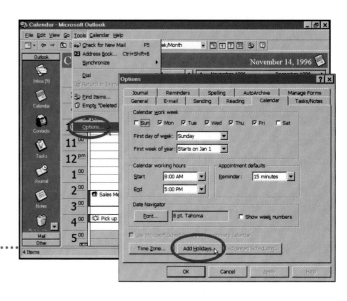

1 Open the **Tools** menu and select **Options**. The Options dialog box appears.

2 Click the **Calendar** tab if necessary. Then click **Add Holidays**.

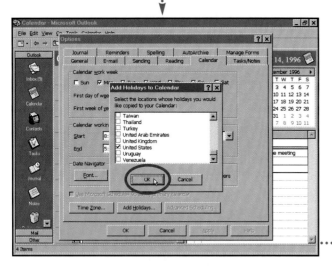

3 The Add Holidays to Calendar dialog box appears. Select the country whose holidays you want to add to your Calendar, by clicking it. You can select more than one country if you like. When you're ready, click **OK**. You'll see a message telling you that you're Calendar's being updated.

Puzzled?

Holidays appear as events in your Calendar—they do not affect your available time. If you need to, you can delete a holiday as you would any other event: Click it and then click the **Delete** button on the Standard toolbar.

4 After the holidays have been added to your Calendar, you're returned to the Options dialog box. Click **OK** to return to Outlook. ■

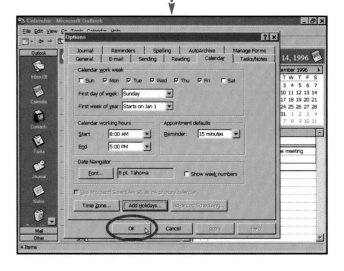

Printing Your Calendar

"Why would I do this?"

You might want to print out your calendar when you plan on being out of the office. You might also want to print it out in order to add it to your day planner.

You can print out any part of your Calendar: a single day, a week, or a month. To get the Calendar printout to fit into your day planner, you may need to change the paper size or orientation. Outlook provides a simple header and a footer (text which prints at the top or bottom of each page) which contains items such as the page number, current date, and your name, but you can add or delete items to suit your individual taste. To see if you'll like your changes, you can preview them before you print.

1 Click a **View** button to display the day, week, or month you wish to print. Open the **File** menu and select **Print**.

2 Select a print style. To print each day, select **Daily Style**. To print seven days, select **Weekly Style**. Print a monthly calendar by selecting **Monthly Style**. With **Tri-fold Style**, each day prints on its own page. Select the range of days you want to print in the **Print range** area. Click **Page Setup**.

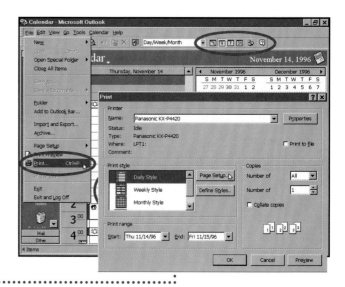

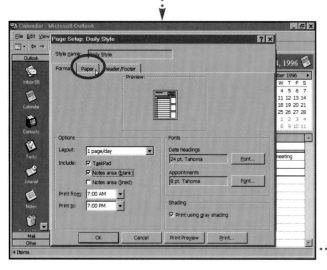

3 The Page Setup dialog box displays with the Format tab in front. In the Layout drop down list, choose the number of days/weeks/months you want printed on a page. From the Include options, choose whether you want to print your tasks and any notes. To change the title font, click the **Font** button, select a font, and click **OK**. Click the **Paper** tab.

4 On the Paper tab, choose the size paper on which to print by selecting it from the **Paper Type** list. To enter a custom paper size, select **Custom** from the list, and enter the **Dimensions** you want. After selecting a paper type, select a layout from the **Page Size** list. An illustration of your selection appears in the right-hand corner of the dialog box. You can also adjust the **Margins** and the **Orientation** if you like. Click the **Header/Footer** tab.

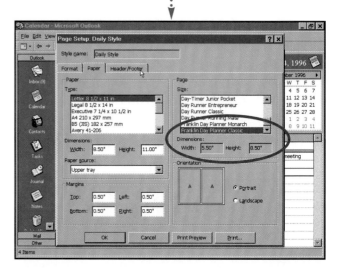

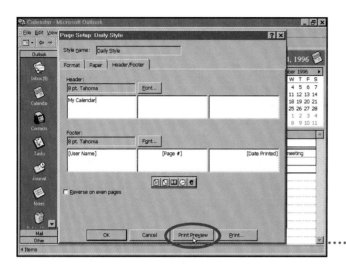

5 To create a header or a footer, enter what you want in the appropriate text box. To insert text, click in the text box and type. To delete an item, select it and press **Delete**. Click the buttons located under the footer area to insert the page number, the total number of pages, the date, the time, or your name where you want them. When you're through, click **Print Preview**.

Missing Link

If you're printing a booklet, click the **Reverse on even pages** option.

6 Here you can see what your printout will look like before you actually print it. If something's wrong, you can return to the Page Setup dialog box by clicking **Page Setup**. When you're ready to print, click **Print**, and you're returned to the Print dialog box.

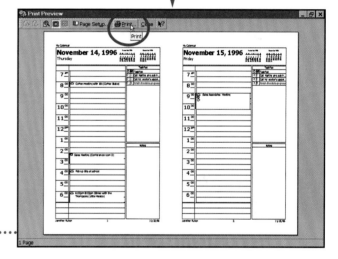

Missing Link

Orientation refers to the direction in which the text prints on the page. In Portrait orientation, text prints across the shortest width of the paper. In Landscape orientation, text prints along the paper's largest width.

7 Click **OK** to print your message(s). ■

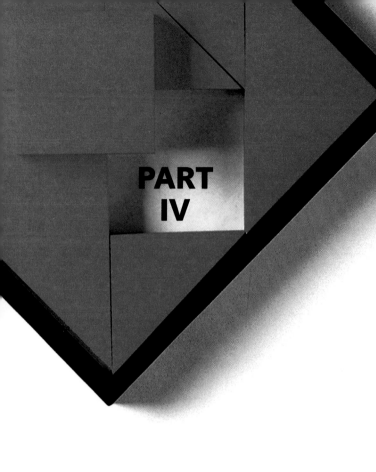

PART IV

Managing Contacts and Address Books

▲ ● ■ ▲ ● ■ ▲ ●

HAVE YOU EVER LOST AN IMPORTANT PHONE NUMBER? Do you jot down addresses, phone numbers, and contact names on whatever happens to be handy? Don't worry—Outlook can help.

The Contact section of Outlook helps you organize phone numbers, addresses, fax numbers, mobile phone numbers, e-mail addresses, and other information about the important people in your life, both personal and professional. Once information is entered into the Contact list, you can use it to send e-mail messages, schedule an appointment, arrange a meeting, delegate a task, visit a client's Web page, and even dial the phone to call a contact.

The Contact list allows you to store all the information you might need on a contact. For example, you can enter both a professional and a personal address for a contact, along with professional and personal phone numbers. You can even enter an extra address as "Other." In addition (and keeping with today's technology), you can enter a mobile phone number, a pager number, a fax number, and several e-mail addresses. You can even enter the address of a person's (or a company's) World Wide Web page. Then (provided you have access to the Internet), you can visit your client's Web page with the click of a mouse.

For important business contacts, you can enter the name of their assistant and their boss, the name of their company and their department, and their official title. But there's room for personal information too, such as a contact's birthday, anniversary, nickname, and spouse's name.

Through Outlook's Journal, you can track conversations with a contact. Then in the Contact list, you can view the conversations and other information entered in the Journal about a particular contact all in one convenient place.

Information in the Contact list can be sorted in various ways. Initially, contact information is displayed in a phone listing, with each contact appearing on a single line, and his professional and personal phone numbers appearing in separate columns. This type of listing is convenient for contacting a person by phone, especially since you can have Outlook dial the phone number for you.

The Contact list can be sorted in other ways as well. If you like the look of a conventional phone book, you can switch to the Address card. In this view, addresses are displayed along with the contact's phone numbers. There's a detailed address listing as well, which displays additional information about each contact.

You can sort the Contact listing by company or location. When your contacts are listed this way, a small minus sign appears next to each company or location's name, with the individual contacts appearing underneath. If you click the minus sign, the contact names for that particular company or location are temporarily hidden, and the minus sign changes to a plus. Click this plus sign, and the contact names are redisplayed.

If you add a category or categories to each contact, then you can sort by it. For example, you might select the categories "Business" or "Personal," in order to arrange your business and personal contacts in different parts of the list. Of course, there are other categories you can use as well, including Key Customer, Competition, Hot Contact, Supplier, and so on. You can also make up additional categories as needed.

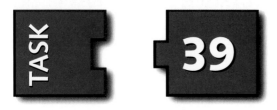

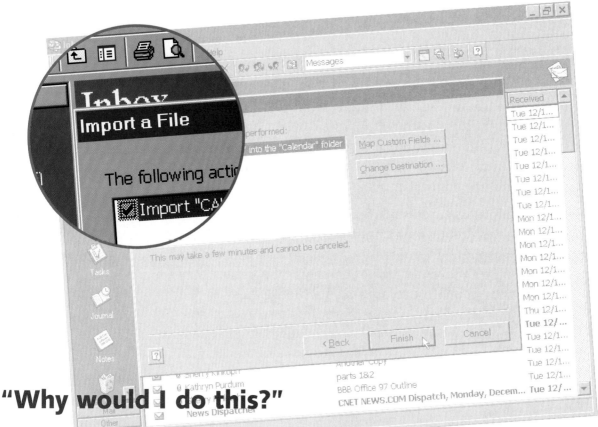

Importing an Old Address List

"Why would I do this?"

If you have been using another electronic day planner such as Schedule+ or Lotus Organizer, you can import your contact names, phone numbers, and addresses into Outlook, without having to retype them.

Outlook can import data from many different types of programs, including Act!, SideKick, ECCO Pro, Microsoft Exchange, Schedule+, and Lotus Organizer. You can even import data from Microsoft Excel or Microsoft Access.

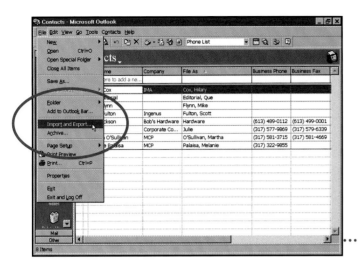

1 Open the **File** menu and select **Import and Export**.

2 The Office Assistant appears. If you'd like help at this time, click **Yes, please provide help**. If you'd like to follow the steps here, click **No, don't provide help now**. Then, in the Import and Export Wizard dialog box, click **Import from Schedule+ or another program or file**. Then click **Next>**.

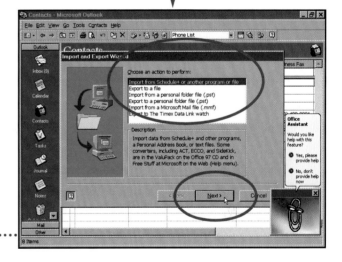

3 Select your program name in the **Select file type to import from** list. Then click **Next>**.

Puzzled?

If you don't see your program listed, a file converter for your program may be contained on the Office CD-ROM. Insert the CD and click **Add/Remove Programs** to install the file converter you need.

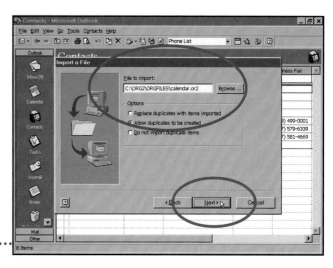

4 Type the path to the file you want to import, or click **Browse**, change to the folder in which the file is stored, select it from the list, and click **OK**. Also, choose how you want duplicates handled. When you're ready, click **Next>**.

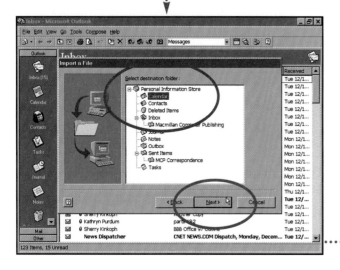

5 Select a destination folder, and click **Next>**.

6 Click the action you want taken, and a check mark appears in front of it. Click **Finish**, and the file is imported into Outlook. ■

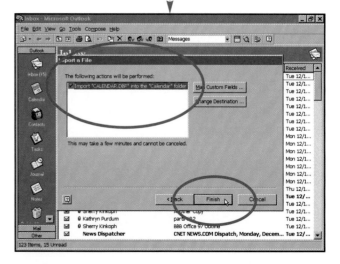

Adding a Contact

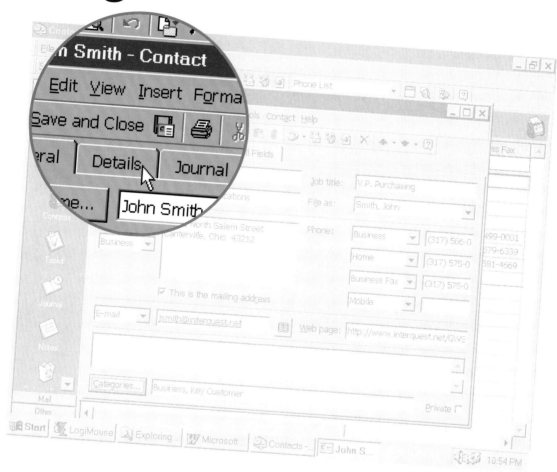

"Why would I do this?"

Everyone has important people in their life—both business and personal. With the Contact list, you can keep track of them all easily. When you add a new contact, it's saved in the Contact Address Book. You may have other address books if you added certain e-mail services to Outlook, such as Microsoft Exchange (Personal Address Book), CompuServe Information Manager, and so on. You can access these address books to copy e-mail information to your new contact.

Task 40: Adding a Contact

1 Click the **New Contact** button on the Standard toolbar.

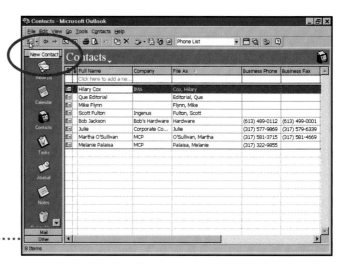

Missing Link

Need to add a new contact for the same company as an existing contact? Just click the existing contact, then open the **Contacts** menu and select **New Contact from Same Company**.

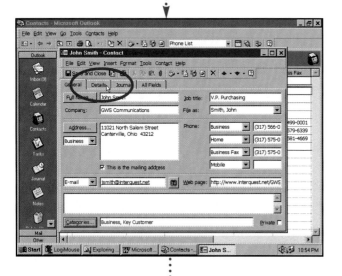

2 In the New Contact dialog box, enter the contact's name, company, job title, and other information. If you want to categorize your contacts, click the **Details** tab.

Puzzled?

If you want to enter a personal address too, just select **Personal** from the **Address** drop-down list. (The Business address will still be saved.) Also, in the phone area, you can enter additional phone numbers by selecting the type of phone number you want to enter from the **Phone** drop-down lists.

3 The Details page is displayed. Enter additional information about a contact. To enter a birthday or anniversary, click the down arrow on the list box, and a calendar appears. Click the date you want. When you're through entering information, click the **Journal** tab.

Missing Link

Create a new contact from an e-mail message by dragging that message from the Inbox to the Contact icon on the Outlook bar.

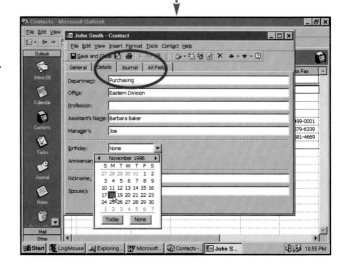

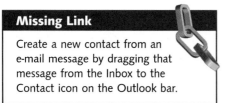

4 On the Journal page, you can track activity related to a contact. Later, you can return to this page to view that activity. To track activity for a contact, click the **Automatically record journal entries for this contact**. Click the **All Fields** tab.

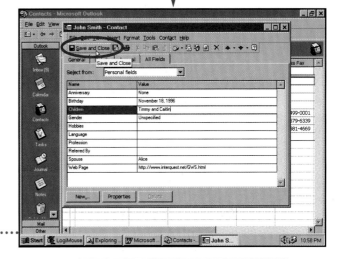

5 On the All Fields page, enter whatever additional information you have about your contact. Select the fields you want to display from the **Select from** list. Once the proper fields are displayed, click a field and type your information. When you're though entering information, click **Save and Close**.

Puzzled?

If you need to enter unique information, you can do so with the User defined fields. To display these fields, select **Miscellaneous fields** from the **Select from** list. Create your own fields by clicking **New,** entering a name for your field, and clicking **OK**.

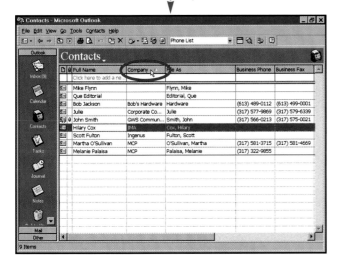

6 The new contact appears in the list. Contacts are normally listed in alphabetical order, sorted by the File As field. To sort on another field, click its header. For example, click the **Company** header. ■

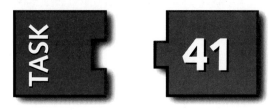

Changing Contact Information

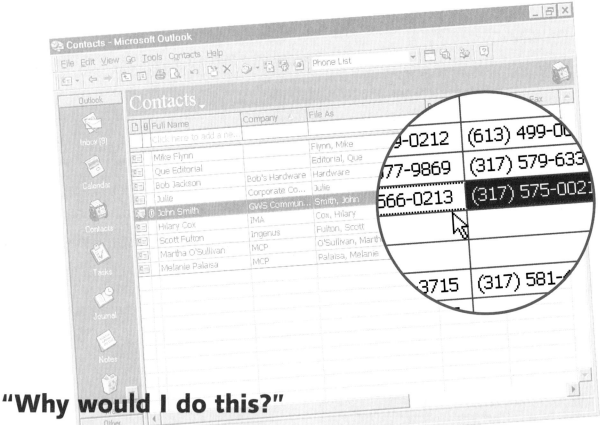

"Why would I do this?"

You may have to change a contact's information for many reasons: the contact's title and position may have changed, his company might have relocated, or his phone number might have changed.

Instead of changing existing data for a contact, you may want to add new information. For example, you might have just found out what your contact's assistant's name is, and now you want to enter it.

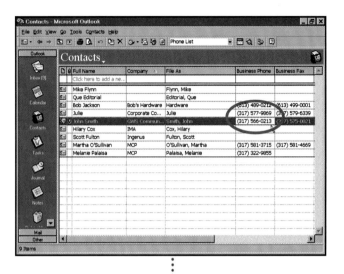

1 Click the contact you wish to change. The contact is highlighted in blue to show that it's selected. To change a field which is visible (such as the contact's business phone number), just click in that field. Press **Backspace** to delete characters to the left of the cursor, or **Delete** to remove characters to the right. Then type your entry. When you're through, click a different entry. Your changes are saved.

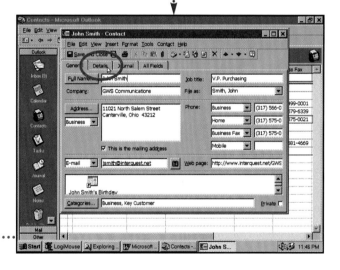

2 If the field you want to change (or add) is not visible, then double-click the contact name. The Contact dialog box appears. Click the tab which contains the field you want to change. For example, click the **Details** tab.

3 Make your changes, then click **Save and Close** to save them. ■

Printing Your Contact List

"Why would I do this?"

You might want to print out your contact list and take it with you when you leave the office. You might also want to print it out in order to add it to your day planner.

You can print out information for one contact, or several. Prior to printing it out, you can select from several options. To see if you'll like your changes, you can preview them before you print.

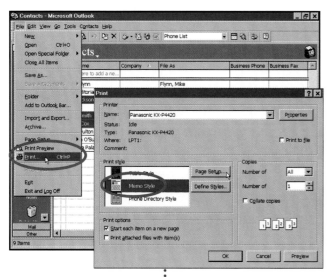

1 If desired, select the contact you wish to print. Open the **File** menu and select **Print**.

2 Select a print style. To print all the information about a contact, select **Memo Style**. To print only the names and phone numbers for each contact, select **Phone Directory Style**. Click **Page Setup**.

3 The Page Setup dialog box appears. On the Format tab you can change the font used. For example, to change the title font, click the **Font** button in the **Title** area, select a font, and click **OK**. Click the **Paper** tab.

Puzzled?

If you're going to fax your contact list, or if you're using a color printer, you may wish to deselect the **Print using gray shading** option.

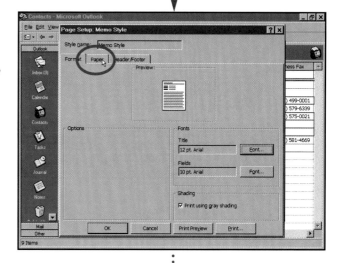

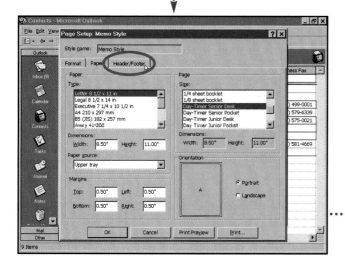

4 On the **Paper** tab, Choose a different size paper on which to print by selecting it from the **Paper Type** list. Once you've selected a paper type, select a layout from the **Page Size** list. You can also adjust the **Margins** and the **Orientation** if you like. Click the **Header/Footer** tab.

5 To create a header or a footer, click in the left, right, or center text box. Then click the buttons located under the footer area to insert the page number, the total number of pages, the date, the time, or your name. When you're through, click **Print Preview**.

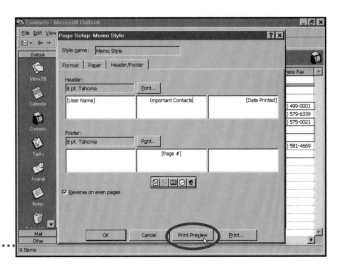

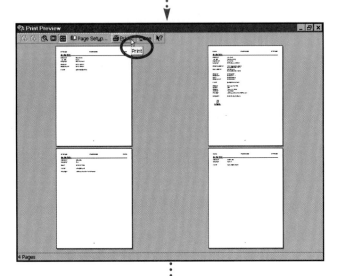

6 In Print Preview, you can see what your printout will look like before you actually print it. To display multiple pages, click the **Multiple Pages** button. When you're ready to print, click **Print**, and you're returned to the Print dialog box.

Puzzled?

If something's wrong with the way the printout looks, you can return to the Page Setup dialog box by clicking **Page Setup**.

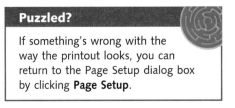

7 Click **OK** to print your message(s). ■

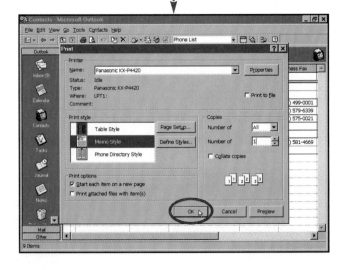

Creating a Distribution List

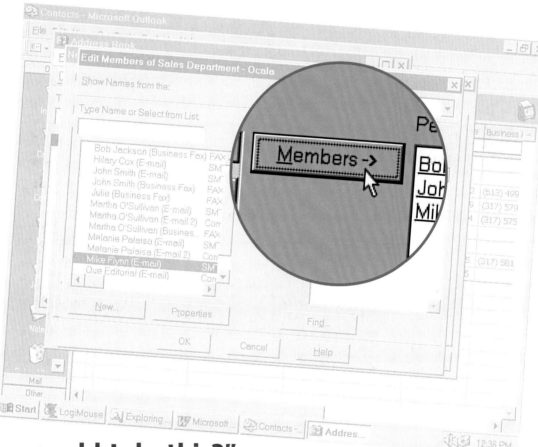

"Why would I do this?"

If you often send e-mail messages to the same small group of people, you can create a special Contact entry for them called a *personal distribution list*. Then, to send the message, instead of selecting each individual person's name, you simply select the distribution list you

created. The names in the list are used to send copies of the message.

You can create multiple distribution lists if needed. For example, you might need a distribution list for everyone in your department, and another one for your fellow managers.

Task 43: Creating a Distribution List

1 Open the **Tools** menu and select **Address Book**.

> ### Puzzled?
>
> As you can see, the process of adding a distribution list is different from adding a new contact. You must use the Address Book window to add a distribution list—it can't be done within the Contact window.

2 The Address Book dialog box appears. Click the **New Entry** button.

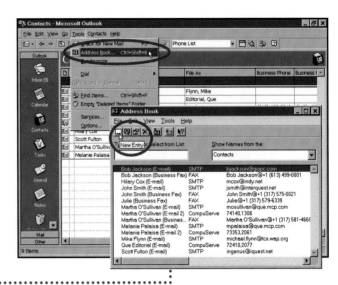

3 At the bottom of the **Select the entry type** list, choose **Personal Distribution List**. Select either Personal Address Book or Contacts from the **In the** list. Click **OK**.

> ### Puzzled?
>
> Since a distribution list is different from a regular Contacts entry, you may want to keep them separated, in the Personal Address Book. However, if you save the list in Contacts, you can drag it to the Inbox icon to create a quick e-mail message. So the choice is yours.

4 In the New Personal Distribution List dialog box, type a **Name** for your new list. Then click **Add/Remove Members**.

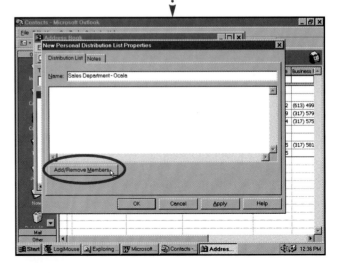

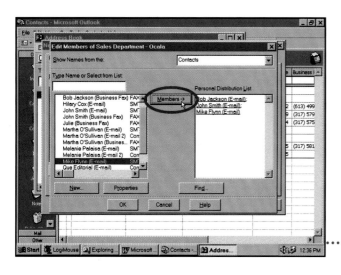

5 Click a name in the list on the left, and click **Members** to add it. Repeat this step to add additional members to your list. When you're through, click **OK**.

Puzzled?

Switch to a different address book if needed by selecting one from the **Show names from the** list.

6 You're returned to the New Personal Distribution List Properties dialog box. The members you selected for your distribution list appear in the large text box. Click **OK** to save your list.

Missing Link

You can add a note about the distribution list (such as the date on which it was last updated) by clicking the **Notes** tab and typing your information into the large text box.

7 Your new distribution list appears in the Address Book window. Click the **Close** button to return to Outlook. ■

Puzzled?

To create an e-mail message using your distribution list, simply click the **New Message** button, click **To**, then select the address book which contains your distribution list from the **Show names from the** list. Click the distribution list name, and click **To**. Then click **OK** to return to the message window.

Phoning a Contact

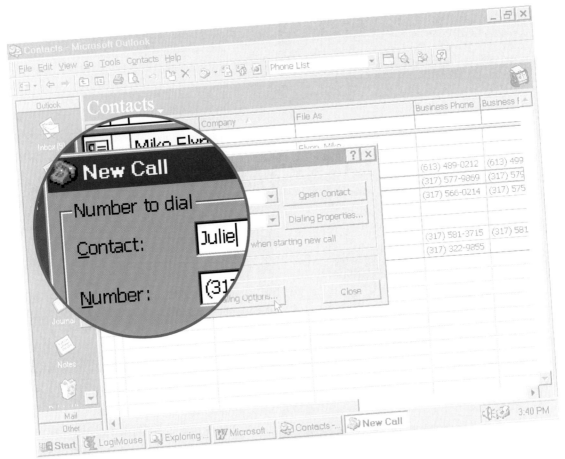

"Why would I do this?"

If you make quite a few phone calls during the day, the process can be quite annoying and repetitive: First, you have to locate the phone number for your contact. Then you have to locate your phone, dial the number, and hope the

phone line isn't busy or that you haven't misdialed. Since you have to open Outlook to look up the number, why not have it dial the phone for you?

In order for Outlook to dial your phone, you must be using the same phone line for both your phone and modem.

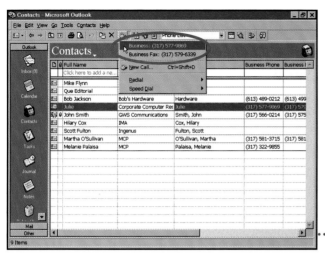

1 Click the **Contacts** icon in the Outlook bar. Click the name of the contact you want to call. Then click the arrow on the **AutoDialer** button. (If you click the AutoDialer button itself, you'll dial the first phone number listed for that contact.) A listing of the contact's various phone numbers appears. Click the one you want to use.

2 In the New Call dialog box, verify that the number you want to dial is correct. You can log the call by clicking **Create new journal Entry when starting new call**. To add frequently dialed numbers to a speed dial list, click the **Dialing Options** button.

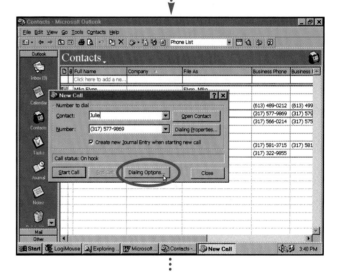

Missing Link

If you normally dial a 9 to get an outside line, you may want to verify that this option has been set up properly under Windows 95. Click **Dialing Properties**, and check the information under the **How I dial from this location** section.

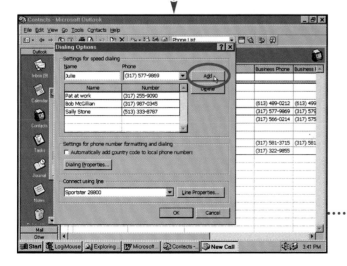

3 Type the contact's name in the **Name** box. The contact's phone number should appear in the **Phone** box. Click **Add**. Repeat to add more names to the list, then click **OK**.

Puzzled?

To use your speed dial list, open the **Tools** menu, select **Dial**, then select **Speed Dial**. Click a number on the list to dial it.

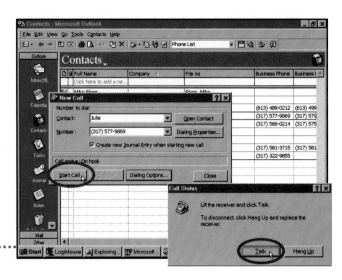

4 When you're ready, click **Start Call**.

5 The modem dials the number. When it connects, lift the receiver on your phone and click **Talk**.

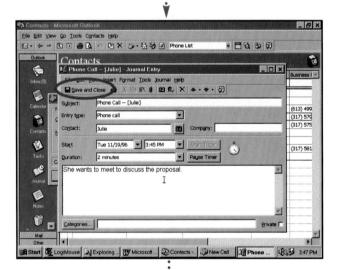

6 If you're recording this call in the Journal, a window appears. Type your notes into the large text box; the duration of the call is automatically logged. Click the **Save and Close** button.

Missing Link

You can select a category for this call by clicking **Categories** and selecting one from the list. Using categories helps you locate and sort items in Outlook.

7 When you're through with the call, click **End Call**. Then click **Close** to return to Outlook. ■

Puzzled?

You can view your journal entry within the Contacts section by double-clicking a contact, then clicking the **Journal** tab.

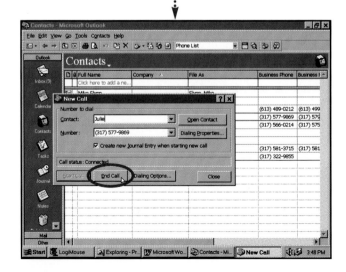

Visiting a Contact's World Wide Web Page

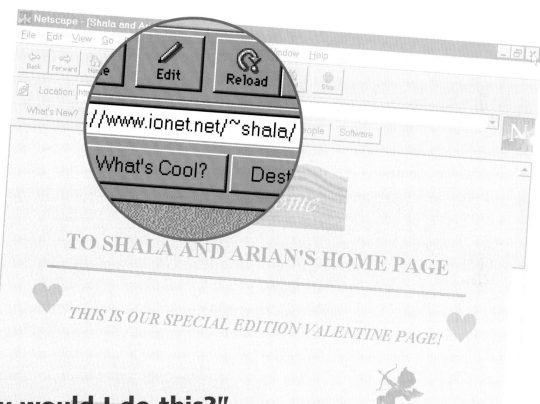

"Why would I do this?"

It seems that just about every business has a World Wide Web page on the Internet. Typically, background, product, and sales information is made available on such pages. If the company of one of your contacts has a Web page, you can use Outlook to quickly connect to it. Also, if your company has an

inter-office intranet, you can connect to a coworker's Web page quickly and easily.

Of course, you'll need a connection to the Internet (or intranet) yourself, and a Web browser such as Netscape Navigator or Internet Explorer to complete this task.

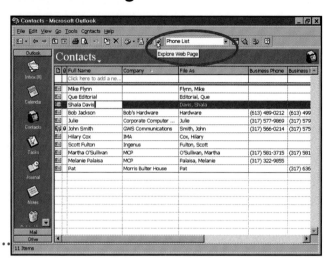

1 First, connect to the Internet (or log onto your company's intranet) in the usual manner. Open the Contacts list and click the contact whose Web page you want to visit. Click the **Explore Web Page** icon on the Standard toolbar.

2 Outlook starts up your Web browser and connects to the Web page you selected. When you're through browsing, click the browser's close button.

3 If you connected to the Internet via modem, then disconnect from the Internet by clicking **Disconnect**. ■

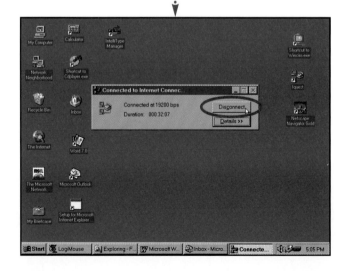

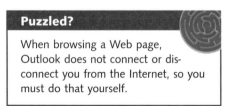

Puzzled?

When browsing a Web page, Outlook does not connect or disconnect you from the Internet, so you must do that yourself.

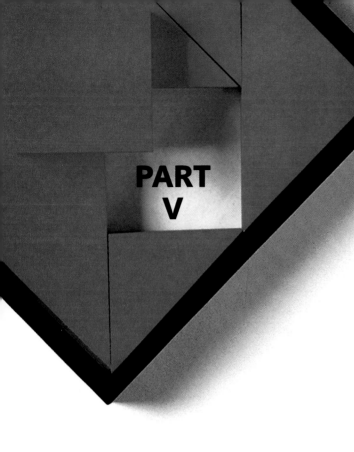

PART V

Keeping Track of Things to Do with the Tasks List

▲ ● ■ ■ ▲ ● ■ ▲ ●

ARE YOU FINDING IT HARD to keep track of all the things you have to do? Well, the Tasks list can help. In the Tasks list, you can enter a task, set a deadline, and even post a reminder so you'll remember to complete the task on time. The Tasks list also keeps track of the tasks you've completed, so you can show your boss what you've been doing with your time.

You can enter both personal and business tasks into the Task List. For example, you might want to be reminded to pick up some milk on the way home, or to drive your son to baseball practice. On the business side, you may have a complex project which requires several tasks to be completed. You can enter all these tasks (complete with deadlines) into the Task list. Then, as you complete each part of the project, you can track your progress. (Completed tasks appear in dull gray at the top of the list, with a line through it.)

Sometimes you won't be able to complete a task on its due date. That's all right—uncompleted tasks automatically appear on the next calendar day, so you won't forget to do them. Overdue tasks appear in red, so they stand out from other tasks which are not past their due dates.

The Tasks list allows you to prioritize your tasks by marking important tasks as "high priority," and relatively unimportant tasks as "low priority." You can then sort by the priority of the tasks to display the most important tasks at the top of the Tasks list. You can also drag tasks up and down the list, to display them exactly where you want them.

When a task is due, it appears in the Calendar for that day. As you finish tasks during the day, you can mark them as completed. You can add tasks directly to the TaskPad which appears in the Calendar, or you can add them through the Tasks list itself.

If you have special tasks which reoccur, you don't have to keep entering them in your calendar over and over. With the Tasks list, you only need to enter a task once—and by specifying the period at which the task repeats, Outlook will enter it multiple times in the Tasks list.

If you're working on a project, the Tasks list can help you track your progress. As you complete each part of the project, you can update the percentage completed. Then, when you glance at the Tasks list, you can easily see the amount of progress you've made. You can also add notes to a task, such as "Waiting on someone else," or "Not started," to explain the amount of progress you've made (or that you haven't made).

If you like to keep your tasks organized, Outlook offers you the ability to categorize them. For example, you might categorize some tasks as personal, and others as business. But it doesn't stop there. If some tasks belong to a particular project, you can categorize them as "Beams Project," or "Company Relocation," for example.

You can also sort your tasks in other ways. For example, you can sort them by their date due, by category, by status, and by percentage complete, among other things.

If a long list of tasks is too confusing, you can display only the current tasks. If you need to check on a past task, you can display only completed tasks. Outlook gives you the freedom to display as much (or as little) detail as you need.

Sometimes you need to reassign a task to someone else. With Outlook, you can send a task request, asking a coworker to complete the task. If he accepts, you can request status reports to update you on his progress. If you are on a company network, status reports can be sent to you automatically, and they can be made to update the percentage completed, as it appears in your Task list.

If you find that you're on the road a lot, keeping track of all the things you need to do can be quite difficult. If needed, you can print out your Tasks list and take it with you. If you use one of the popular day planners, such as a Franklin Day Planner, Day Timer, and so on, you can print out your list in a format which will fit it.

Adding a Task

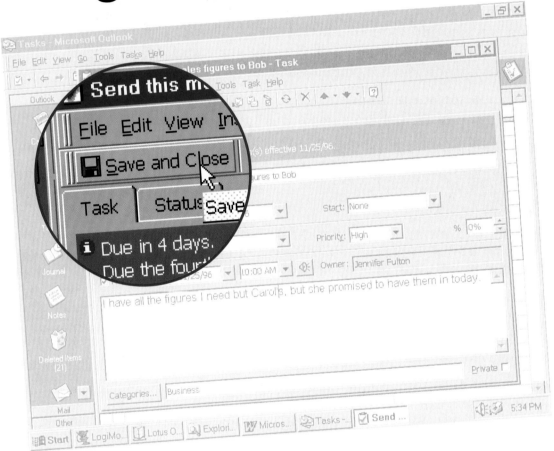

"Why would I do this?"

If you want to keep track of something you need to remember to do, you can add it to the Tasks list. When you add the task, you can specify a due date. You can also be reminded when the task is due, so you won't forget to do it on time.

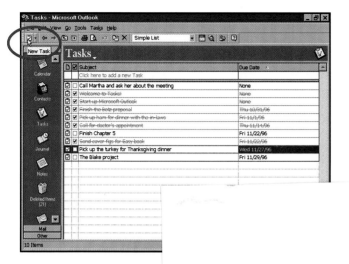

1 If you're in the Tasks list, click the **New Task** button to add your task. If you're in the Calendar, you can add a task directly to the TaskPad which appears there.

Missing Link

If you just want to add something to the Tasks list, and you ~~w~~ant to specify a due date ~~or~~ other option, you can click the **~~He~~re to add a new Task** place~~holder. J~~ust type a description and ~~press En~~ter to add the task.

2 Type a description ~~in the~~
Subject text box. ~~Set a due date~~
by opening the Du~~e list and selecting a~~
date. Select a **Prio~~rity~~**
for the task if you ~~like. You can add~~
a note explaining t~~he task to yourself~~
in the large text bo~~x, and even insert a~~
file by clicking the

Puzzled?

To move from month to month in the Due calendar, click the left or right arrow which appear at the top of the calendar window.

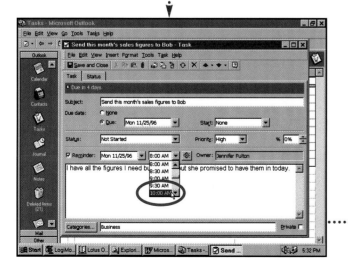

3 If you'd like to be reminded of the task's due date, click **Reminder**. Then select a date and time from the lists.

Missing Link

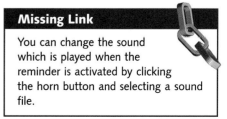

You can change the sound which is played when the reminder is activated by clicking the horn button and selecting a sound file.

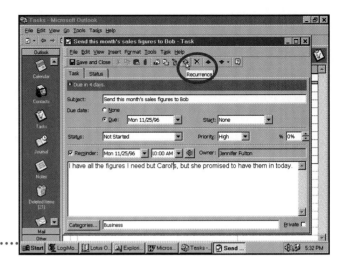

4 If the task reoccurs at regular intervals, click the **Recurrence** button.

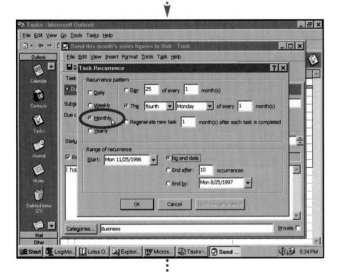

5 In the **Recurrence pattern** area, select the frequency you want. In the **Range of recurrence** area, you can set a limit to the number of times the task is copied to your Calendar. Click **OK**.

Puzzled?

If you want the task to be copied to several dates in your Calendar, choose a **Recur every XX** option.

6 Click **Save and Close**. The task is added to the list. ■

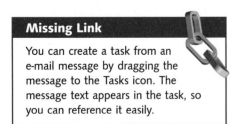

Missing Link

You can create a task from an e-mail message by dragging the message to the Tasks icon. The message text appears in the task, so you can reference it easily.

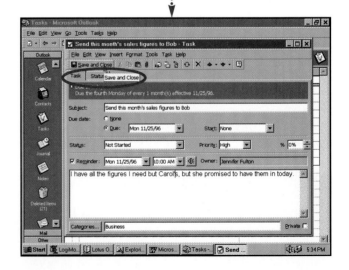

Printing the Tasks List

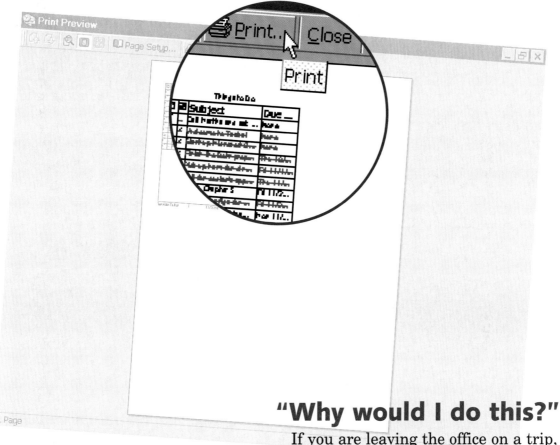

"Why would I do this?"

If you are leaving the office on a trip, you might want to print out your Tasks list and take it with you. You can even print it out in a format which will allow you to add it to your day planner.

You can print out the tasks for one day, a week, a month, and so on, simply by selecting the tasks you want to print. You'll also be able to select from several options and to preview them before you print.

Task 47: Printing the Tasks List

1 Select tasks by pressing and holding the **Ctrl** key as you click them. If they are listed together, press **Shift**, click the first task you want to select, then click the last task. Open the **File** menu and select **Print**.

2 Select a print style. In the **Print range** area, click **All items** if you want to print the entire Tasks list. Memo Style prints each task on its own page. You can also print attached files. Click **Page Setup**.

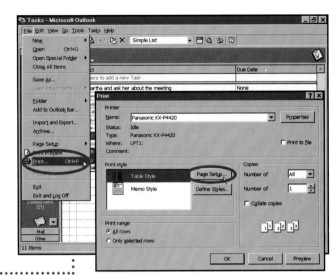

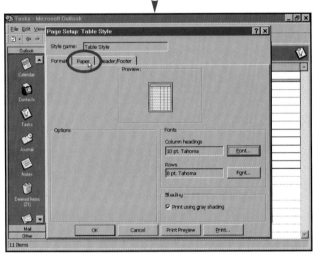

3 On the Format tab you can change the font used. For example, to change the title font, click the **Font** button in the **Column headings** area, select a font, and click **OK**. Click the **Paper** tab.

Puzzled?

If you're going to be faxing your task list to someone, or if you have a color printer, you may wish to deselect the **Print using gray shading** option.

4 On the Paper tab, choose the paper size from the **Paper Type** list. Enter a custom paper size by selecting **Custom** from the list, and then enter the **Dimensions** you want. Now select a layout from the **Page Size** list. An illustration of your selection appears. Adjust the **Margins** and the **Orientation**, if you like. Click the **Header/Footer** tab.

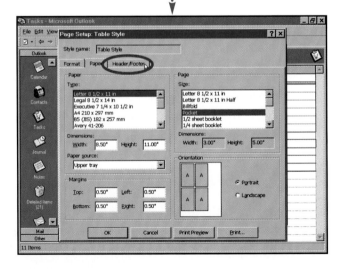

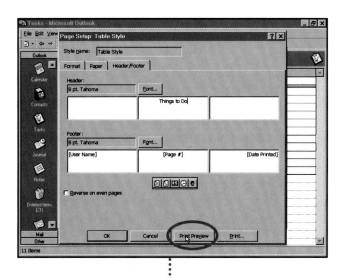

5 To create a header or footer, enter the text in the appropriate text box. For example, notice that in the footer, your name will print on the left, the page number in the middle, and the date on the right. To insert text, simply click in the text box and type. To delete an item, select it and press **Delete**. The buttons located under the footer area enable you to insert the page number, the total number of pages, the date, the time, or your name. When you're through, click **Print Preview**.

6 Here you can see your printout before you actually print it. To display multiple pages, click the **Multiple Pages** button. When you're ready to print, click **Print**, and you're returned to the Print dialog box.

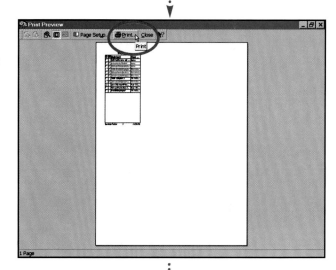

Puzzled?

If something's wrong with the way the printout looks, you can return to the Page Setup dialog box by clicking **Page Setup**.

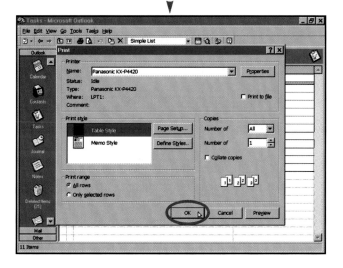

7 Click **OK** to print your task(s). ■

Missing Link

If you're printing a booklet, click the **Reverse on even pages** option.

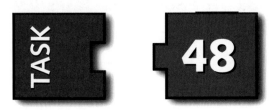

TASK 48

Assigning a Task to Someone Else

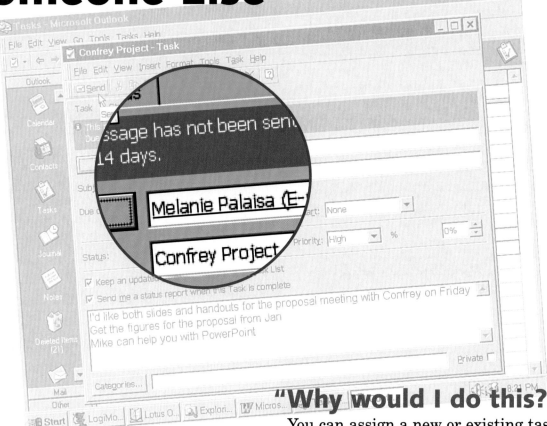

"Why would I do this?"

You can assign a new or existing task in your list to someone else, by sending a task request. The recipient of the request has the option of accepting the task, reassigning the task to someone else, or declining it.

You can keep a copy of the original task in your list and receive updates as to its status. If you don't keep a copy, you can still receive a report when the task is completed.

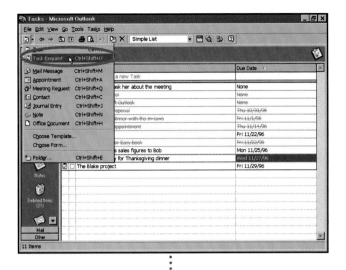

1 To create a request for a new task, click the down arrow on the **New Task** button and select **New Task Request**. Skip to Step 3. If you want to reassign an existing task, then double-click it to open it, and continue to Step 2.

Puzzled?

You can only assign a task to someone located on your company network who is also using Outlook.

2 Click the **Assign Task** button on the Standard toolbar.

Puzzled?

If the task is declined by the person to whom you assigned it, you can reassign it to someone else by opening the task and clicking **Assign Task**.

3 Type the e-mail address to the assignee in the **To** box. Also type a description in the **Subject** text box. Select a **Due date** and a **Priority**. Type notes you have about the task in the large text box. If you're reassigning an existing task, make the changes that are needed.

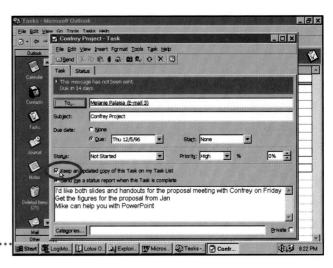

4 If you want to keep a copy of the task, select **Keep an updated copy of the Task on my Task List**. As progress is made on the task, Outlook will notify you automatically.

5 Whether or not you kept a copy of the task, you can receive a final status report when the task is marked complete. Click **Send me a status report when this Task is complete**.

6 When you're ready, click **Send**. ■

Puzzled?

If you want to reassign this task to someone else after it was accepted, you can, as long as a copy of it still appears in your Tasks list. Simply open the task and the **Status** tab, and click **Create unassigned copy**. Click **OK**. Then repeat these steps to reassign the task to someone else.

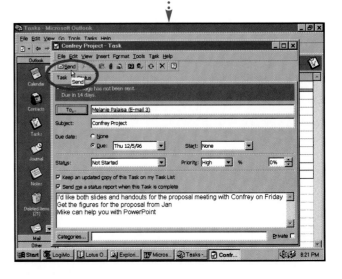

Responding to a Task Request

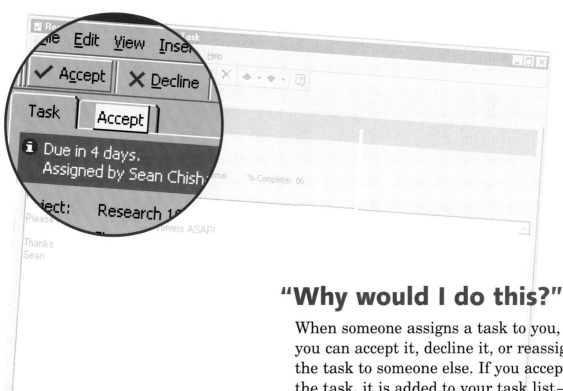

"Why would I do this?"

When someone assigns a task to you, you can accept it, decline it, or reassign the task to someone else. If you accept the task, it is added to your task list—at that point, you're the only person who can make changes to the task or update its status.

When you update the status of the task, a copy of it may be automatically sent to the person who originated the task (if that person requested it). In any case, when you complete the task, a status report is automatically sent to the task's originator.

159

Task 49: Responding to a Task Request

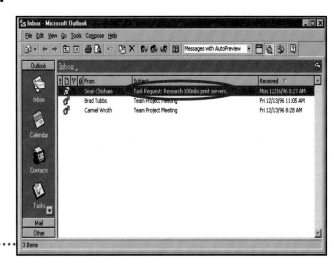

1 Double-click the message which contains the task request in order to open it.

2 Click either **Accept** or **Decline**.

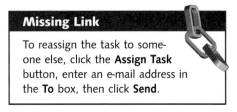

Missing Link

To reassign the task to someone else, click the **Assign Task** button, enter an e-mail address in the **To** box, then click **Send**.

3 If you don't want to add a comment to your reply, click **Send the response now.** If you'd like to add a comment, click **Edit the response before sending**, and type your response in the large text box. Click **Send.** ■

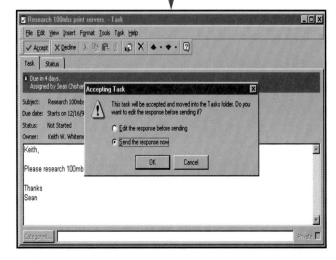

Sending the Status of a Task

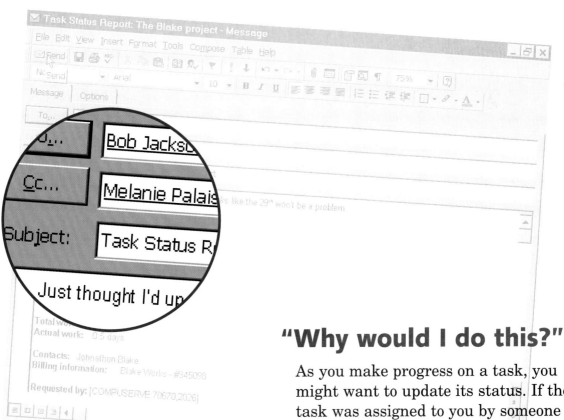

"Why would I do this?"

As you make progress on a task, you might want to update its status. If the task was assigned to you by someone else, it's important that you keep the status of the task current, because the task originator may be receiving automatic updates.

Even if the task is your own, if you update its status, you can quickly check your progress on a project by glancing at the Tasks list.

1 Double-click the task whose status you wish to update. The task opens.

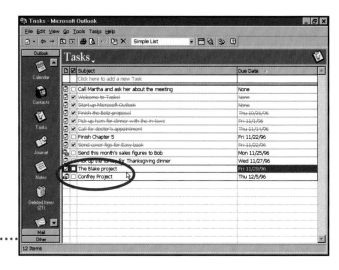

Missing Link

If you simply want to mark a task as complete, click the **Complete** box. A check mark appears, and the task is crossed out.

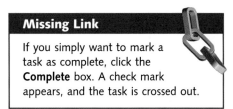

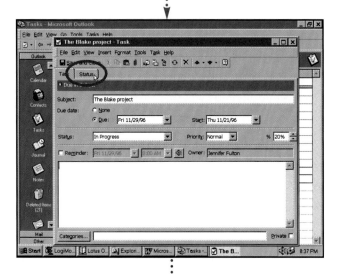

2 Select a **Start** date. Then select an option under **Status**, such as "In Progress," or "Waiting on someone else." If you've completed a part of the task, you can mark the percentage complete with the % spinner. Click the **Status** tab.

Missing Link

To view the status of a task or the percentage complete while in the Tasks list, select the **Detailed List** option from the **Current View** box in the Standard toolbar.

3 On the Status tab, enter the total number of hours the task is expected to take, along with the number of hours you've actually spent on it. Enter additional information which applies, such as **Mileage** and **Billing information**. If you don't want to send a status report to anyone, click **Save and Close**.

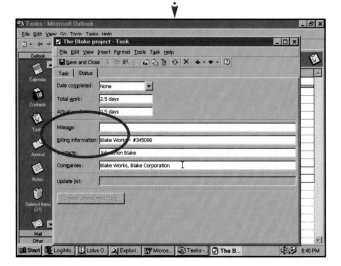

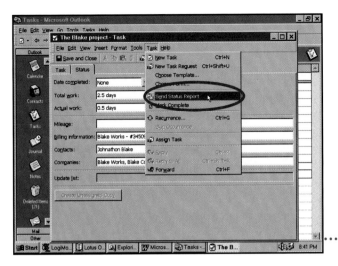

4 Open the **Tasks** menu and select **Send Status Report.**

Missing Link

You can send a copy of the task to someone by clicking **Forward**. The task is included in the resulting e-mail message as an attachment.

5 Enter the addresses to which you want the status report sent in the **To** or **Cc** boxes.

Puzzled?

If the task was assigned to you, the appropriate names may already be entered in the **To** box.

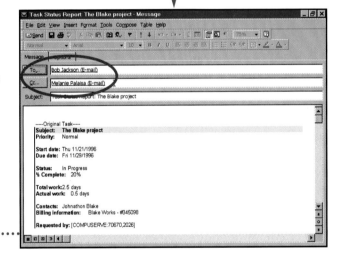

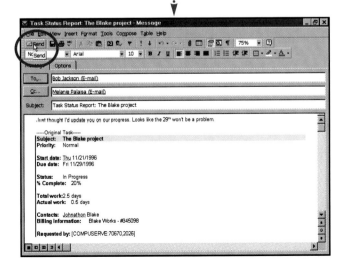

6 Click **Send.** ■

Puzzled?

Completed tasks are not removed from the Task list. If you want to delete a task from the list, click it and then click the **Delete** button.

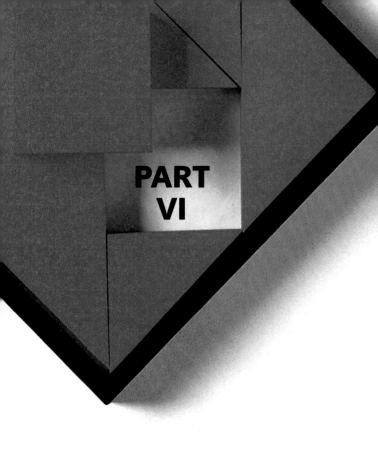

PART VI

Creating and Maintaining a Journal

WITH THE JOURNAL, YOU CAN MAINTAIN a record of all your activities. You can record phone calls, meeting notes, time spent on projects, and so on.

Items that you create within Outlook can be tracked in the Journal. For example, you can track all the e-mail messages, faxes, and files that you sent or received from a particular client. And so you don't clutter the Journal with information you don't need, you can specify the contacts whose activities you want the Journal to track.

Outlook also can track the work that you do with Microsoft Office. Want to know when you last updated the budget worksheet in Excel? Check the Journal. Want to see if you wrote that letter to Mr. Billings? Check the Journal. Since certain activities are recorded for you automatically, maintaining your Journal is easy.

When you need to, you can add your own entries to the Journal. For example, you might want to record the minutes to a meeting, or a conversation you had with a client over lunch.

Certain Outlook activities can not be recorded automatically in the Journal. For example, appointments are not recorded, and neither are tasks. However, meeting requests and task requests sent to you by a coworker can be automatically recorded as well as phone calls which you initiate from within Outlook. In any case, any activity which is not recorded automatically can be recorded manually.

The entries in the Journal can be sorted various ways. For example, you can sort each entry by its date, in order to view your activities on a particular day. You can also sort the entries by category, such as Business and Personal. Or you can sort the entries by type, to view all your phone calls in one place, for example.

Automatically Recording Your Activities

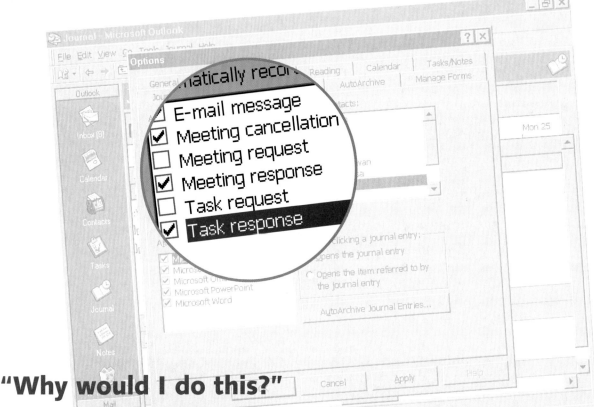

"Why would I do this?"

Although you can record activities in the Journal manually, why not let Outlook do some of the work for you? Outlook can track the items you create which are related to particular clients. Then, when you switch to the Journal, you can view all the items related to a client in one place.

Outlook can also track the documents you create using Microsoft Office—such as letters, memos, and reports created with Microsoft Word, worksheets created with Excel, databases maintained in Access, and presentations created with PowerPoint.

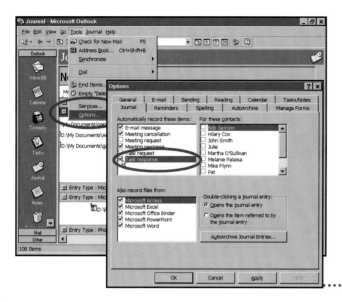

1 Switch to the Journal by clicking the **Journal** icon in the Outlook bar. Open the **Tools** menu and select **Options**.

2 Under **Automatically record these items**, select the Outlook items you want the Journal to record. The items you select appear with a check mark.

Puzzled?

If you decide that you no longer want to track an item, click it again to remove the check mark.

3 Select the contacts for which you want these items recorded in the **For these contacts** box.

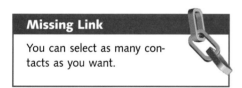

Missing Link

You can select as many contacts as you want.

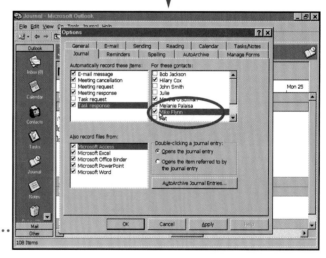

4 Under **Also record files from**, select the Microsoft Office programs whose activities you want automatically recorded in the Journal. Click **OK**.

Puzzled?

The activities you selected will be recorded *from now on*. To record previous activities, you must enter them into the Journal manually.

169

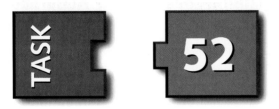

Entering Activities Manually

"Why would I do this?"

Although Outlook tracks a lot of activities for you automatically, there are many activities which it does not track. These activities you can enter into the Journal manually. For example, you might want to record the details of a conversation you had with a client over dinner. Or you might want to record the details of an appointment.

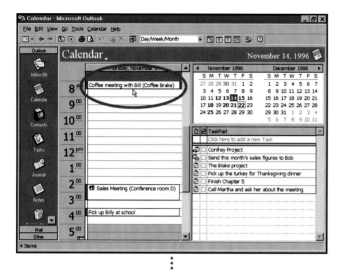

1 If the item you want to record is an Outlook item (such as an appointment or a meeting), open the item by double-clicking it.

Missing Link

To create a Journal entry quickly, simply drag the item onto the Journal icon on the Outlook bar. For example, drag the appointment from the Calendar to the Journal.

2 Open the **Tools** menu and select **Record in Journal**.

3 If needed, you can add or change any of the information related to the activity. When you're through, click **Save and Close**.

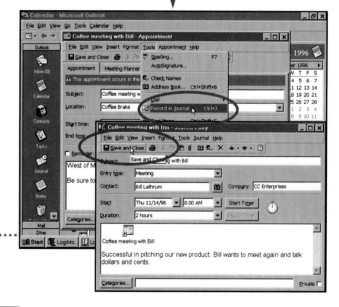

4 To record a document in the Journal, open Explorer and drag its icon into the Journal window.

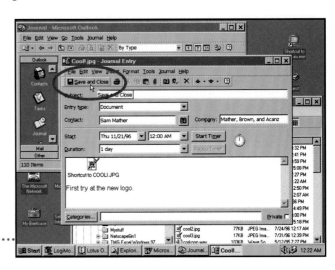

5 Enter a description of the document in the **Subject** box. Select the type of entry you're recording in the **Entry type** box. Enter other information which applies, such as a **Contact** name. When you're through, click **Save and Close**.

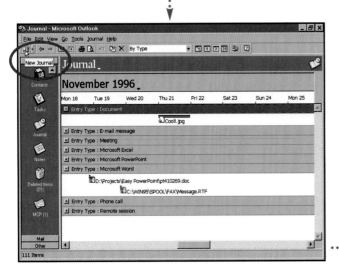

6 To record other entries in the Journal, click the **New Journal** button.

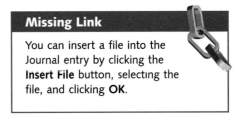

Missing Link

You can insert a file into the Journal entry by clicking the **Insert File** button, selecting the file, and clicking **OK**.

7 Enter a description of the activity in the **Subject** box. Select the type of entry you're recording in the **Entry type** box. Enter other information which applies, such as a **Start** time and **Duration**. You can add a note or comment in the large text box. Click **Save and Close**. ■

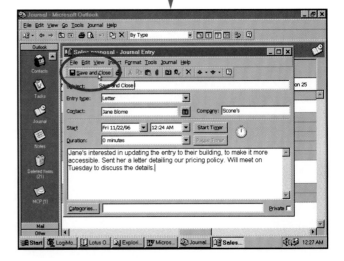

Viewing Entries in the Journal

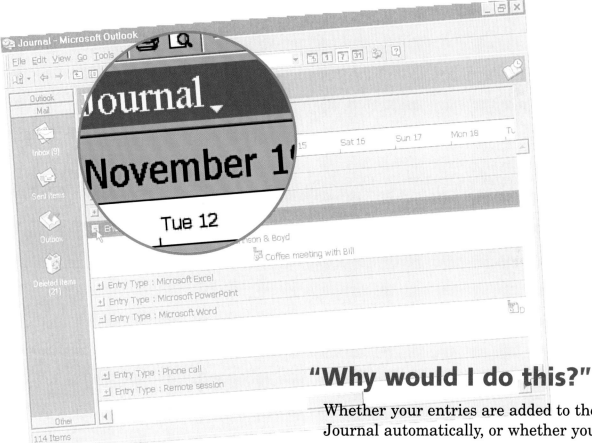

"Why would I do this?"

Whether your entries are added to the Journal automatically, or whether you add them yourself, you'll want to review them at some point. Outlook lets you sort the entries by type, contact, and company, among others. Sorting the entries allows you to locate the ones you wish to review quickly.

1 Initially, the Journal entries are grouped by type. To display the items in a group, click the **plus sign**. The list expands to display its contents. To hide the list again, click its **minus sign.**

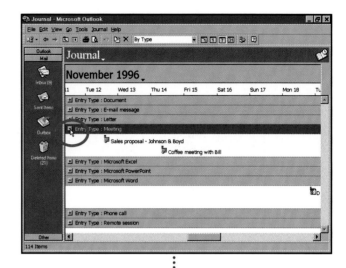

Missing Link

Normally, activities for the week are displayed in the Journal. You can display a day's, or even a month's activities by clicking the **Day** or the **Month** button.

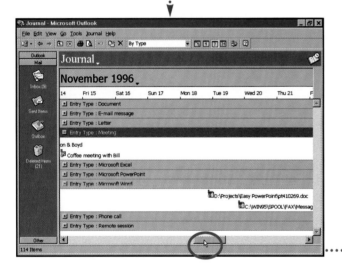

2 Items in the Journal are listed under the day they occurred. To view a day which is not currently visible, use the scroll bars.

Puzzled?

To jump directly to a particular day, click the **Timeline** banner (on the word **November**, for example) and a calendar appears. Click the date of the activities you wish to view.

3 You can change how items are grouped and displayed by selecting a viewing option from the **Current View** list. If you made changes to the current view, you may see a warning asking if you'd like to save them. Click **Yes** to save the changes, or **No** to discard them. ■

Missing Link

You can view just the most recent activities by selecting **Last Seven Days** from the **Current View** list.

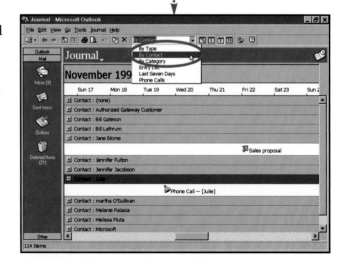

Printing Your Journal

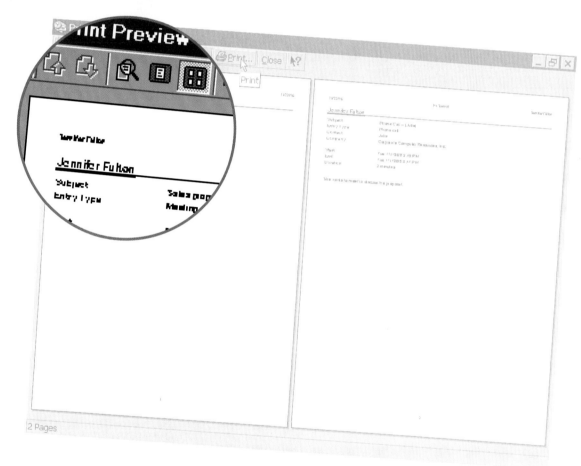

"Why would I do this?"

In the Journal, you keep a record of various activities, including phone calls, document changes, meetings, appointments, and so on. You may want to print this record if you're meeting with a client, for example.

The Journal can sort your activities by contact, by type, and by category. Having all your activities relating to a particular client or event all together, makes it easy to produce a paper printout for your files.

Task 54: Printing Your Journal

1 Select the activities you wish to print by pressing and holding the **Ctrl** key. Open the **File** menu, and select **Print**.

2 Activities are printed in **Memo Style.** In **Print options**, select to print each task on its own page if you want. Print attached files by clicking **Page Setup**.

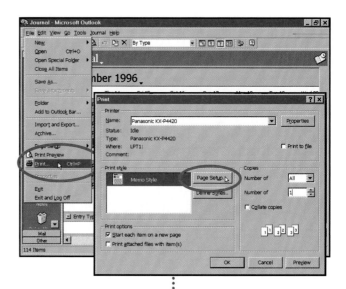

> ### Missing Link
> Print multiple copies by selecting the number from the **Copies** area.

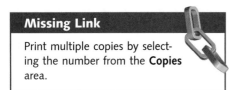

3 On the **Format** tab you can change the font used. For example, to change the title font, click the **Font** button in the **Title** area, select a font, and click **OK**. Click the **Paper** tab.

> ### Puzzled?
> If you're going to bc faxing your journal to someone, or if you have a color printer, you may wish to deselect the **Print using gray shading** option.

4 On the **Paper** tab, choose the paper size by selecting it from the **Paper Type** list. Enter a custom size by selecting **Custom** from the list, and by entering the **Dimensions** you want. Once you've selected a type, select a layout from the **Page Size** list. An illustration appears in the right-hand corner of the dialog box. You can also adjust the **Margins** and the **Orientation** if you like. Click the **Header/Footer** tab.

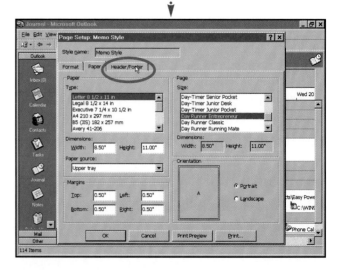

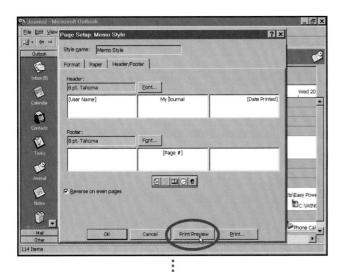

5 To create a header or a footer, enter what you want in the appropriate text box. For example, you'll notice that in the footer, the page number prints in the middle. To insert text, simply click in the text box and type. To delete an item, select it and press **Delete**. The buttons located under the footer area enable you to insert the page number, the total number of pages, the date, the time, or your name where you want them. When you're through, click **Print Preview**.

6 Here you can see what your printout will look like before you actually print it. To display multiple pages, click the **Multiple Pages** button. When you're ready to print, click **Print**, and you're returned to the Print dialog box.

> **Puzzled?**
>
> If something's wrong with the way the printout looks, you can return to the Page Setup dialog box by clicking **Page Setup**.

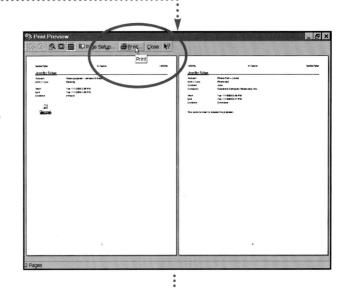

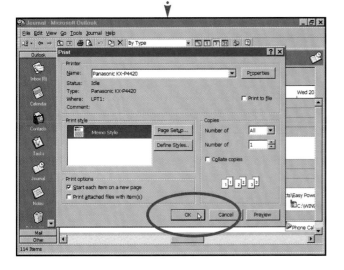

7 Click **OK** to print your Journal entrie(s). ■

> **Missing Link**
>
> If you're printing a booklet, click the **Reverse on even pages** option.

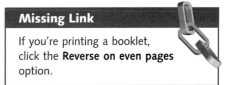

Opening Files Listed in the Journal

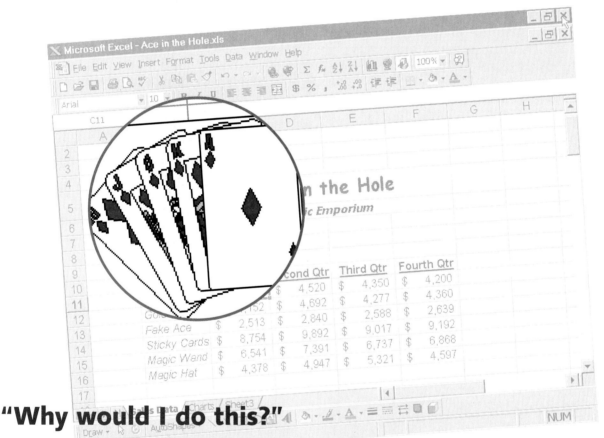

"Why would I do this?"

One of the nicest features of the Journal is that it allows quick access to your files. So rather than switching from Outlook to Explorer or the Start menu to locate a recently used document, why not go straight to the Journal, and open the document from there?

Also, because the Journal maintains a record of your activities each day, you can quickly locate documents you haven't used recently.

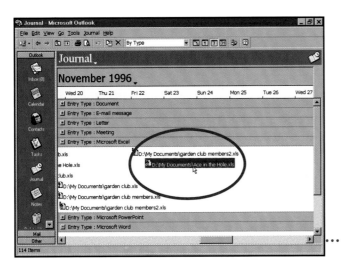

1 Double-click the document you want to open.

Puzzled?

Only Office documents are automatically listed in the Journal, although you can add other documents to the Journal by dragging them there.

2 In the Journal window, double-click the document icon.

Missing Link

If you'd like to be able to open a document by double-clicking it in the Journal, then open the **Tools** menu, select **Options**, click the **Journal** tab, and select the **Opens the item referred to by the journal entry** option.

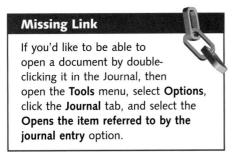

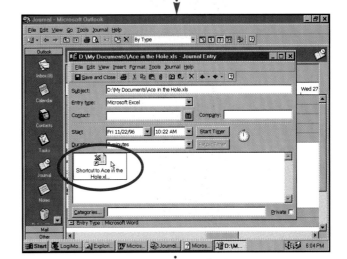

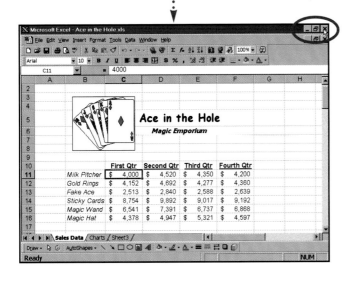

3 Outlook starts the related program, which opens the document. After making any changes, save them, and then click the program's **Close** button to exit the program and return to Outlook. ■

Missing Link

You can also open an Outlook item listed in the Journal by following these steps.

Keeping Track of Small Notes

NSTEAD OF CONSTANTLY MISPLACING important bits of information that you used to jot down on whatever was handy, such as a bit of paper, or a sticky note, why not record them in the Notes section of Outlook? In Notes, you can record quick thoughts, directions to a client's office, small reminders, questions you want to remember to ask, and other items. And, you'll always know where you can find that important piece of information.

Notes appear on-screen looking like paper sticky notes. However, you can also display the notes (and their contents) in a long text list.

You can organize your notes by category (such as business or personal). You can also organize notes by color. For example, you might use yellow for general business-related notes, pink for personal notes, green for notes relating to your latest project, and so on.

Notes are like any other Outlook item: If you need to forward them to someone, you can simply drag a note onto the Inbox icon and send it as an attachment to a message. Or you can drag notes to the Journal to track them.

This process also works in reverse: If you want to create a note relating to a particular appointment, meeting, or e-mail message, simply drag it onto the Notes icon in the Outlook bar. A Note window will open, and the contents of your message or the details of your appointment or meeting appear. You can add your comment above this text.

Want to create a note on a particular contact? Well, just drag the person's name from the Contact list onto the Notes icon. Type your note and close the Notes window to save it.

When you create a note, it's automatically stamped with the current date and time. That way, when you open the note later on, you'll be able to tell exactly when you wrote it. In addition, when viewing your notes, you can opt to display only the notes created in the last seven days if you want.

You can even print your notes if you like. When you print them, you can print just one note, all the notes, or a selection. You also have options on how you want them printed, such as in a long list, or on separate pages.

Creating a Note

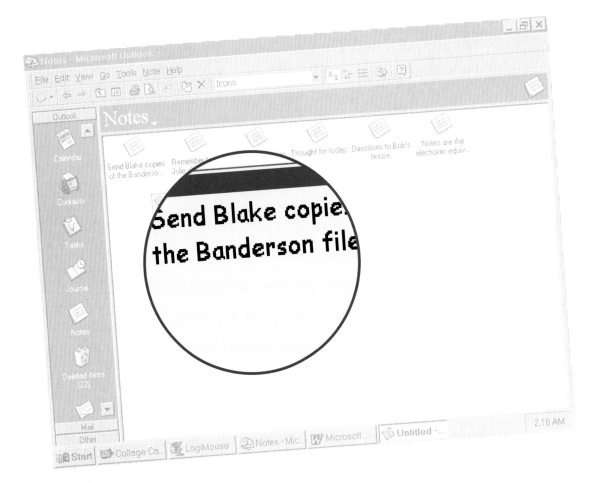

"Why would I do this?"

Notes are like the electronic equivalent of sticky notes. In Notes, you can jot down questions or answers you don't want to forget, important directions, things to remember, a classy quote, or any small bit of information you deem important.

By adding your notes to Outlook, you won't run the risk of misplacing them. Also, you can organize them easily.

1 Click the **New Note** button. A note window opens.

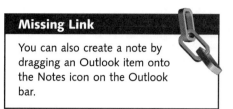

2 Type your thought into the note window. You can copy text from a file by using the Edit, Copy and Edit, Paste commands.

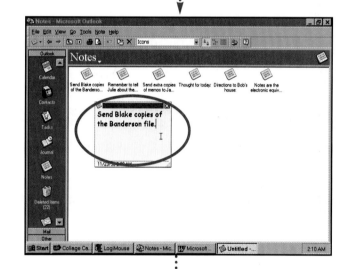

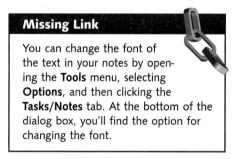

3 You can leave the note open if you like, or close it by clicking its **Close** button. ■

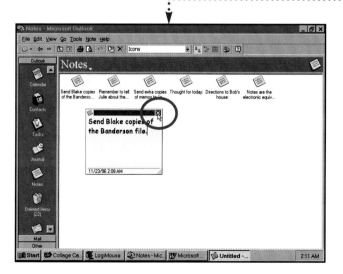

Organizing Your Notes

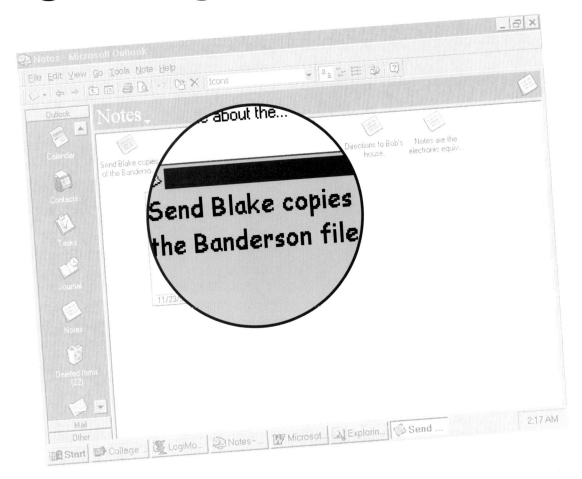

"Why would I do this?"

Outlook lets you organize your notes in several ways. For example, you can add categories to your notes just like you can to other Outlook items, and then sort by this category.

You can also categorize your notes with color. You can make all the notes related to a particular client blue. For another client, you might choose green; for another, yellow. The choice is yours to make.

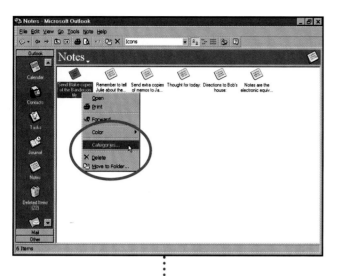

1 Right-click the note you want to change. A shortcut menu appears. Select the option you want to change, such as **Category** or **Color**.

Puzzled?

If the note is open, you can still display the shortcut menu. Simply click the note icon which appears in the upper left corner of the window.

2 If you selected **Category** from the pop-up menu, the Category dialog box appears. Click the categorie(s) that apply. Click **OK**.

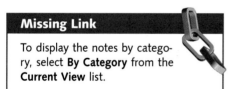

Missing Link

To display the notes by category, select **By Category** from the **Current View** list.

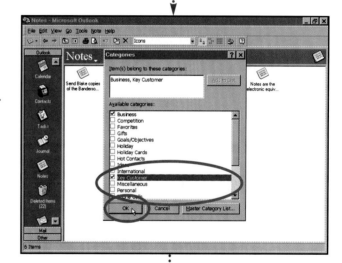

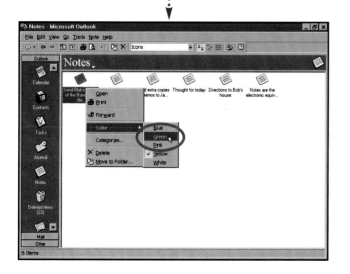

3 If you selected **Color** from the pop-up menu, a cascading menu appears. The current color of the note is displayed with a check mark. Click another color to select it. ■

Missing Link

To arrange your notes by their color, select **By Color** from the **Current View** list.

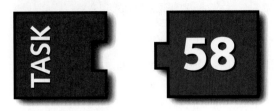

TASK 58

Printing a Note

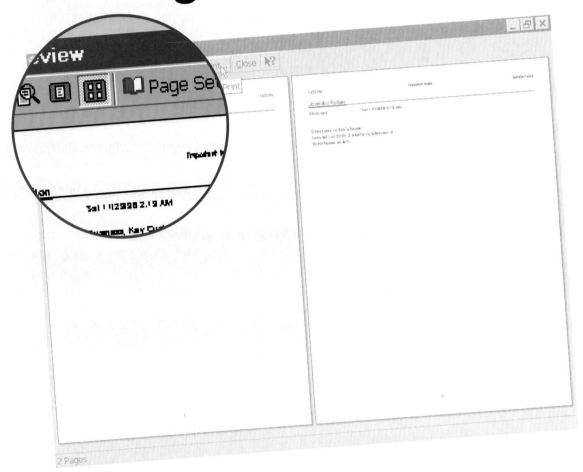

"Why would I do this?"

With Notes, you can keep track of the important bits of your life: a quick question, a conversation in the hall, a change you want to remember to make. If the note involves a client, you may want to print it out in order to keep it with your other records. Or, if the note contains directions, you might want to print them out so you can refer to them in the car.

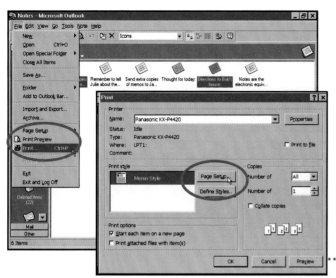

1 Select the note(s) you wish to print, by pressing and holding the **Ctrl** key as you click them. Open the **File** menu and select **Print**.

2 All notes are printed in the **Memo Style**, which print the complete text in each note. In the **Print options** area, select to print each note on its own page if you like. You can also print any attached files related to the note. Click **Page Setup**.

3 On the **Format** tab you can change the font used. For example, to change the title font, click the **Font** button in the **Title** area, select a font, and click **OK**. Click the **Paper** tab.

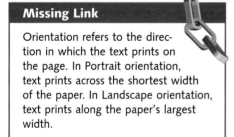

Missing Link

Orientation refers to the direction in which the text prints on the page. In Portrait orientation, text prints across the shortest width of the paper. In Landscape orientation, text prints along the paper's largest width.

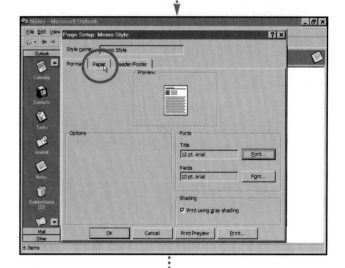

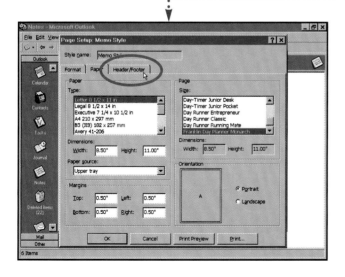

4 On the **Paper** tab, you can choose a different size paper on which to print by simply selecting it from the **Paper Type** list. You can enter a custom size by selecting **Custom** from the list, and entering the **Dimensions** you want. Once you've selected a paper type, select a layout from the **Page Size** list. An illustration of your selection appears in the right corner of the dialog box. You can also adjust the **Margins** and the **Orientation** if you like. Click the **Header/Footer** tab.

189

5 To create a header or a footer, enter what you want in the appropriate text box. For example, you'll notice that in the footer, the page number prints in the middle. To insert text, simply click in the text box and type. To delete an item, select it and press **Delete**. The buttons located under the footer area enable you to insert the page number, the total number of pages, the date, the time, or your name where you want them. When you're through, click **Print Preview**.

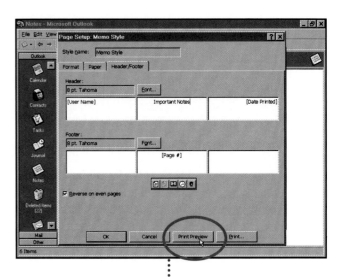

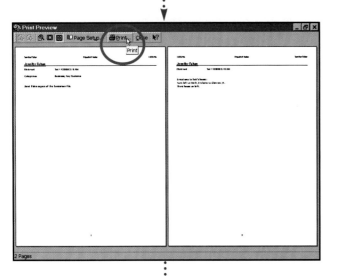

Missing Link

If you're printing a booklet, click the **Reverse on even pages** option.

6 Here you can see what your printout will look like before you actually print it. To display multiple pages, click the **Multiple Pages** button. When you're ready to print, click **Print**, and you're returned to the Print dialog box.

Puzzled?

If something's wrong with the way the printout looks, you can return to the Page Setup dialog box by clicking **Page Setup**.

7 Click **OK** to print your message(s). ■

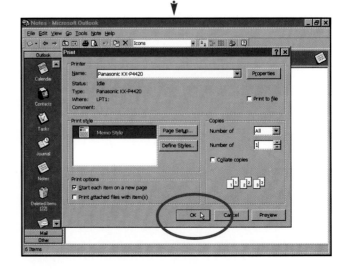

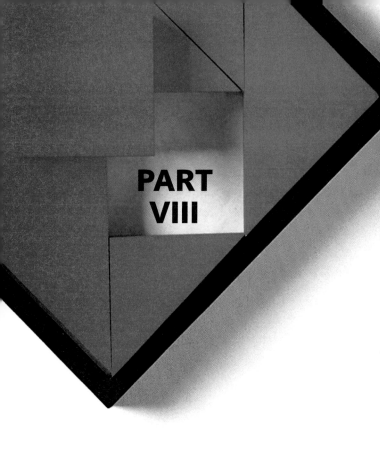

PART VIII

Deleting, Organizing, and Locating Your Outlook Items

THE OBJECTS THAT YOU CREATE in Outlook are all called items. An item, therefore, might be an e-mail message, an appointment, a meeting, a contact, a task, a journal entry, or a note.

The procedures for working with items in Outlook are the same, regardless of what that item is. For example, to delete an old e-mail message, you follow the same steps for deleting an appointment. Since the procedures for managing your Outlook items are the same throughout the program, those procedures are presented together in this part for easy reference.

Here, you'll learn how to delete items you no longer need. You'll also learn how to organize the items you keep. For example, you might want to create a folder for particular types of correspondence, and then copy or move items into the folders you create.

If you don't want to delete a particular item, but you'd like to move it out of the way, then you can *archive* it. When Outlook archives an item, it stores it on your hard disk, but removes it from the Outlook window. If you find you need items that have been archived, you can retrieve them into Outlook. You can also purge (delete) items even after they've been archived.

Outlook provides many ways in which you can organize your items. As I mentioned earlier, you can create new folders wherever they're needed. For example, you might create a folder in the Inbox called Carter Project, and then move all related correspondence to that folder. The Carter Project folder would appear as a subfolder within the Inbox folder itself.

Or, instead of placing your folders within the Inbox, you could create a new group, and place that on the Outlook bar. For example, you might create the Sales group. Sales would then appear as an icon on the Outlook bar. Within the Sales group, you could then create any subfolders you need, such as "The Blakely Company," to help you further organize your sales-related e-mail.

Categories are another way in which you can organize your Outlook items. Outlook comes with many different categories already defined for you, such as "business" and "personal." However, you can add your own categories as well, such as "tax-related." Once you've defined your categories, you can assign them to items as you create them (or after the fact, if need be), and then use these categories to locate or print a particular group of related Outlook items.

But what if you need to locate a particular item, such as the proposal you sent Bill last week? Well, just like in a word processor where you can search for a bit of text, you can search your Outlook items based on their content.

And once you've found the item or items you were looking for, you can copy, delete, or move them as needed. You can even print the items you've found, if you wish. If you find that you work often with the files in a particular folder, you can add a shortcut to that folder in the Outlook bar. This helps you gain quicker access to the files you need as you work.

When working with items, you may find it helpful to display only the information you need. You can do this in several ways. For example, in Contacts, the fields Full Name, Company, File As, Business Phone, and so on. are displayed for each item. You can select which fields you want to display—for example, you might want to display each contact's e-mail address. You can also choose not to display the fields you don't need, such as the File As field.

If you work with large numbers of items, you might want to *group them*. In the Journal, items are automatically grouped for you. You can use this same grouping technique in other parts of Outlook. When items are grouped together, you can display all the items in a group, or you can hide them. Thus, grouping gives you the freedom to display only the items you need to see.

An alternative to grouping is *filtering,* in which the list of items is sent through a filter, which removes the items you don't want to display. For example, in the Inbox, you might filter the items to display only e-mail messages related to the upcoming company relocation project.

Creating Folders to Organize Items

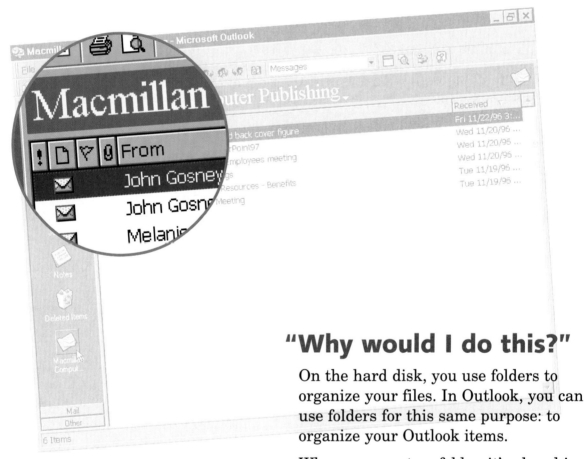

"Why would I do this?"

On the hard disk, you use folders to organize your files. In Outlook, you can use folders for this same purpose: to organize your Outlook items.

When you create a folder, it's placed in the current Outlook section. For example, if you're in Sent Items, and you create a folder called Faxes, then Faxes becomes a subfolder within the Sent Items folder.

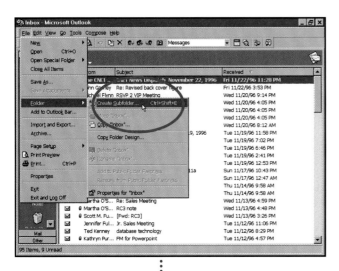

1 Change to the Outlook section in which you want to create a subfolder. For example, click the **Inbox** icon to change to the Inbox. Open the **File** menu and select **Folder**. Then select **Create Subfolder** from the cascading menu that appears.

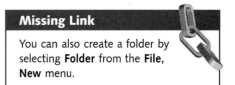

Missing Link

You can also create a folder by selecting **Folder** from the **File, New** menu.

2 Type a **Name** for the folder. Under **Make this folder a subfolder of,** make sure the folder you want to place this folder in is selected. Type a description for this new folder. If you want to to access the folder from the Outlook bar, make sure the option, **Create a shortcut to this folder in the Outlook Bar** is selected. Click **OK**.

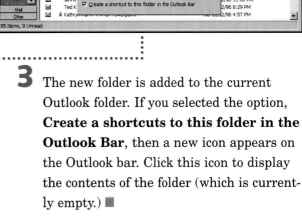

Puzzled?

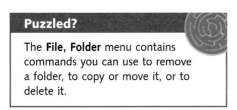

The **File, Folder** menu contains commands you can use to remove a folder, to copy or move it, or to delete it.

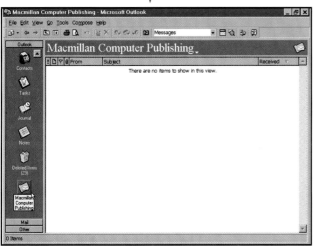

3 The new folder is added to the current Outlook folder. If you selected the option, **Create a shortcuts to this folder in the Outlook Bar**, then a new icon appears on the Outlook bar. Click this icon to display the contents of the folder (which is currently empty.) ▪

Puzzled?

If you didn't select the Create a shortcut option, then, to display the contents of the new folder, click the **Folder banner** to display the folder list.

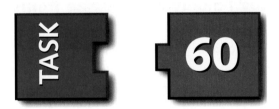

Deleting, Copying, and Moving Items

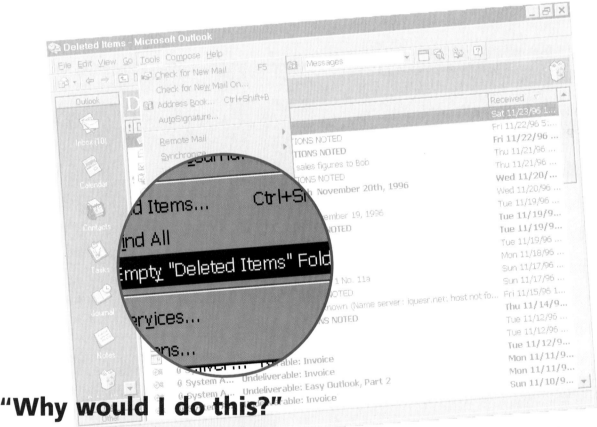

"Why would I do this?"

After you create a folder or two, you'll want to copy or move your Outlook items into these folders, in order to organize them.

When items are no longer needed, you can delete them from Outlook. Deleted items are not actually removed; instead they are moved to the Deleted Items folder. This allows you the chance to retrieve an accidentally deleted item. From time to time, you'll want to empty this folder to permanently delete your unused items.

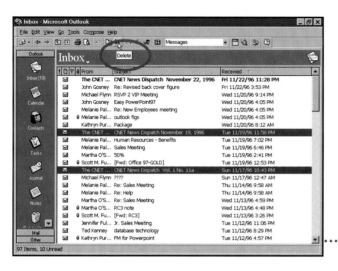

1 Select the item to be deleted by clicking on it. To select multiple items, press **Ctrl** as you click them. Then click the **Delete** button on the Standard toolbar.

Puzzled?

To retrieve an accidentally deleted item *before* it's removed from the Deleted Items folder, right-click it and select **Move to Folder**. Select the folder in which you want the item placed, and click **OK**.

2 Deleted items are moved to the Deleted Items folder. To permanently remove these items, open the **Tools** menu and select **Empty Deleted Items** folder.

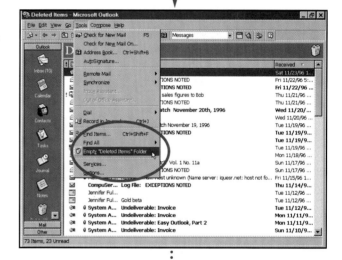

Puzzled?

You can perform Step 2 from any Outlook section; you don't have to view the Deleted Items folder to empty its contents—although you might want to, in order to double-check its contents before you permanently remove them.

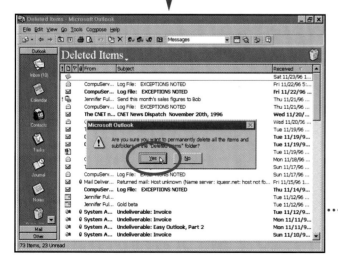

3 You'll see a message asking you if you want to empty the Deleted Items folder. Click **Yes**.

4 To copy or move an item, click it to select it. You can select multiple items by pressing **Ctrl** as you click them. Open the **Edit** menu. Then, to copy the selected items, click **Copy to Folder**. To move the items instead, click **Move to Folder**.

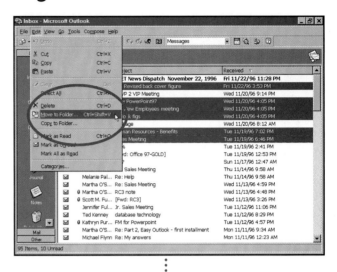

Puzzled?

If you want to make a copy of an item to create a new item that is similar, use the **Edit, Copy** and **Edit, Paste** commands. To create a copy of a contact, use the **Contacts, New Contact from Same Company** command.

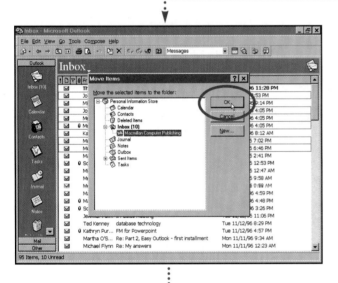

5 Select the folder where you want to copy or move the selected item(s). If needed, click the **plus** sign in front of a folder to display its subfolders, then click the subfolder you want. Click **OK**.

Missing Link

You can create a new folder by clicking the **New** button, typing a name for the folder, and clicking **OK**.

6 The items are copied or moved into the folder you selected. ■

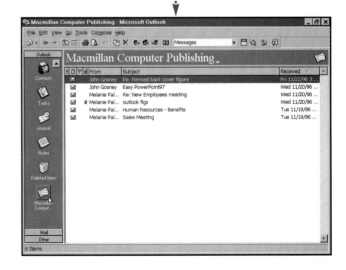

Missing Link

You can copy items quickly by selecting them, pressing **Ctrl**, and dragging them to the folder to which you want to copy them. To move the files instead, *do not press Ctrl* as you drag.

Archiving Important Items

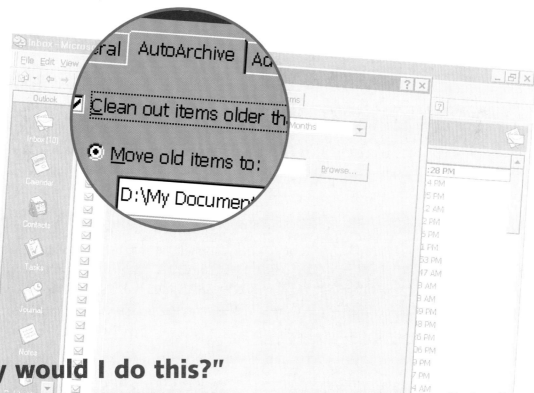

"Why would I do this?"

When an item is archived, it's saved in a special folder on your hard disk, and deleted from Outlook. Think of archiving as a process which clears out old junk from within Outlook. But unlike deleting old items (which removes them permanently), if you need to, you can always retrieve items from the archive later on.

Items in the Calendar, Tasks, Journal, Sent Items, and Deleted Items folders are automatically archived, although you can turn AutoArchive on for other folders, such as Inbox. You can also turn off the AutoArchive feature and archive only the items you wish to keep.

Task 61: Archiving Important Items

1 To turn AutoArchive on (or off) for a particular folder, right-click its icon on the Outlook bar. Select **Properties** from the pop-up menu.

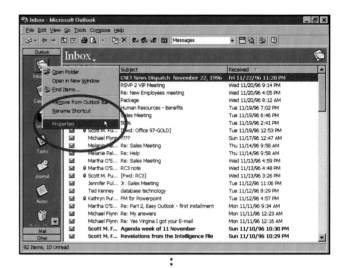

Missing Link

By default, AutoArchive occurs at the following times: Calendar (6 months), Tasks (6 months), Journal (6 months), Sent Items (2 months), and Deleted Items (2 months).

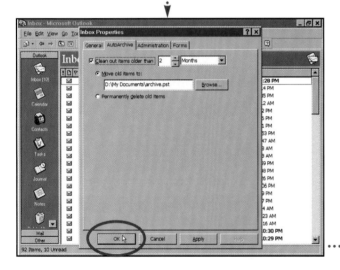

2 Click the **AutoArchive** tab. Select **Clean out items older than XX**, and set the number of months you want items in the folder to be archived. Type the name of the file into which you want the items saved in the **Move old items to** text box, or simply accept the default, which is **archive.pst**. Click **OK**. Items in the selected folder are archived automatically, after the period of time you've selected has passed.

Missing Link

To delete old items without archiving them, select the **Permanently delete old items** option.

3 If you don't want to archive items automatically, then turn off the AutoArchive feature. Open the **Tools** menu and select **Options**.

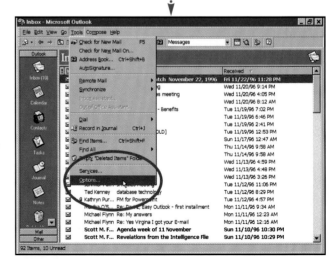

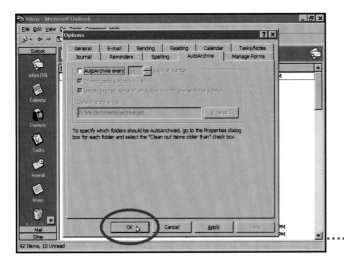

4 Click the **AutoArchive** tab. Click the **AutoArchive every XX option** to turn it off. Click **OK**.

> **Puzzled?**
>
> If you don't run AutoArchive off, you can customize it to your needs with the other commands you'll find on the AutoArchive tab.

5 With AutoArchive turned off, you can still archive files manually. Open the **File** menu and select **Archive.**

> **Puzzled?**
>
> You can set an item so that it is not archived by right-clicking it, selecting **Properties**, and then selecting the **Do not AutoArchive** option.

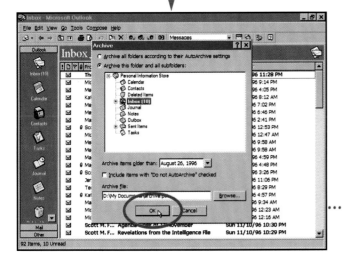

6 To archive all folders, select **Archive all folders according to their AutoArchive settings**. Otherwise, select the folder you want to archive, and click the **Archive this folder and all subfolders** option. Select the date you want to use for archive purposes, and click **OK**.

Task 61: Archiving Important Items

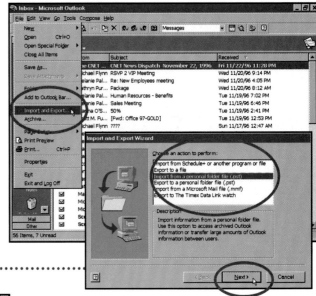

7 To retrieve archived items, open the **File** menu and select **Import and Export**.

8 Select **Import from a personal folder file (.pst)**. Click **Next>**.

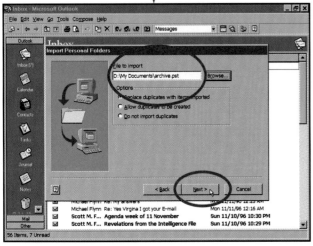

9 Click **Browse,** select the archive file you want to import, then click **Open**. Click **Next>**.

10 Select the folder you want to import, and click **Finish**. The items in the folder you selected are imported into their old folder. ■

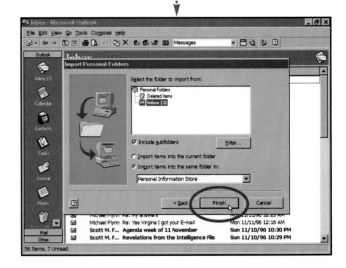

Puzzled?
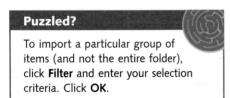

To import a particular group of items (and not the entire folder), click **Filter** and enter your selection criteria. Click **OK**.

Using Categories to Organize Items

"Why would I do this?"

When you assign categories to your items, you can use these categories to help you identify items of a particular type. For example, you might want to separate all your personal contacts from your business ones—and you can, simply by selecting the proper category for each contact.

Outlook allows you to add categories of your own. For example, you might want to add the category, "Vanderholf Project," and use it to identify items related to the project.

Task 62: Using Catagories to Organize Items

1 Click the item to which you want to assign a category. Open the **Edit** menu, and select **Categories**.

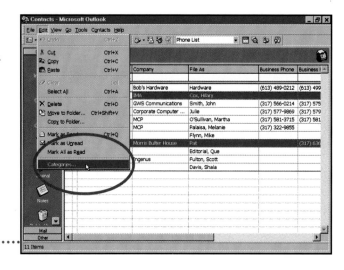

Missing Link

You can assign the same category to multiple items at one time. Press **Ctrl** and click the items to select them.

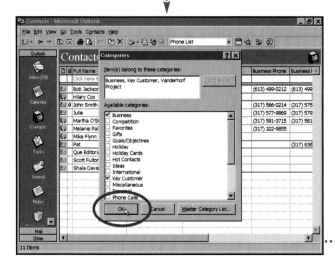

2 To assign a category to an item, click a category to select it. You can assign multiple categories to an item if you like. When you're through, click **OK**.

Puzzled?

If you don't see a category you like, you can create a new one by typing its name in the **Items belong in these categories** text box. Click **Add to List**.

3 The items you selected appear with the appropriate categories. ■

Puzzled?

If the Categories field isn't visible, you can make it appear. Open the **View** menu, select **Show Fields**, select **Categories**, then click **Add**. Click **OK**.

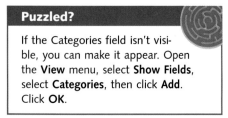

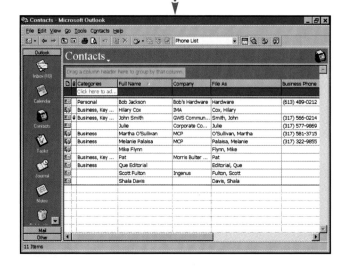

Grouping Items

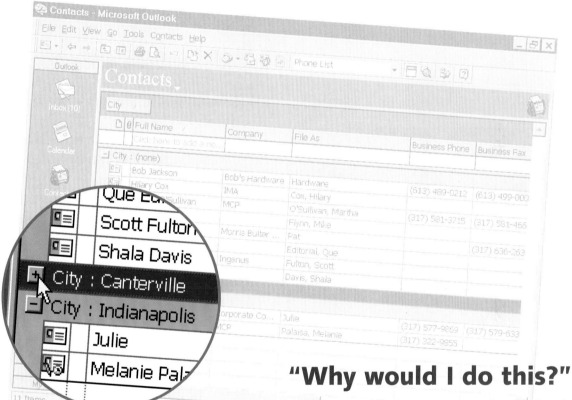

"Why would I do this?"

You can group items in order to display a collection of related items. For example, if you assign categories to your Outlook items, you can use grouping to sort like items together.

You can group items by more than just their categories. For example, in the Contacts list, you might want to group people by their state or their zip code.

Task 63: Grouping Items

1 Open the **View** menu and select **Group By.**

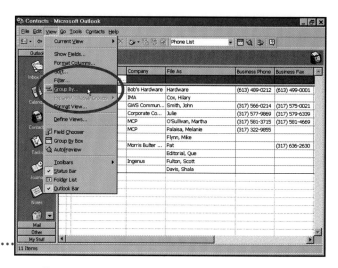

Puzzled?

To sort items based on their icon, select **Group by Box** from the **View** menu.

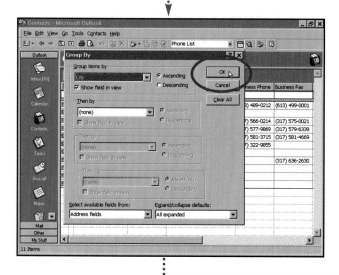

2 Select the field you want to use to group the items from the **Group items by** drop-down list. (If needed, select the category for the field you need from the **Select available fields from** list.) Select **Ascending** or **Descending** order. To display the field you selected, click **Show field in view**. Repeat this step to group items by additional fields. Click **OK**.

Puzzled?

Ascending order displays items in alphabetical order (A to Z). Descending order displays items in reverse order (Z to A).

3 Initially, items are displayed within their groups. To hide the contents of a group, click its **minus sign.** To display the items again, click the **plus sign**. ■

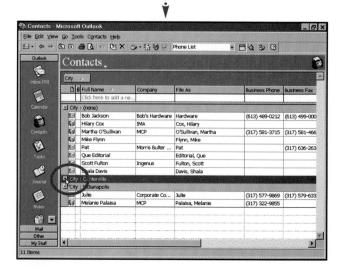

Searching for a Particular Item

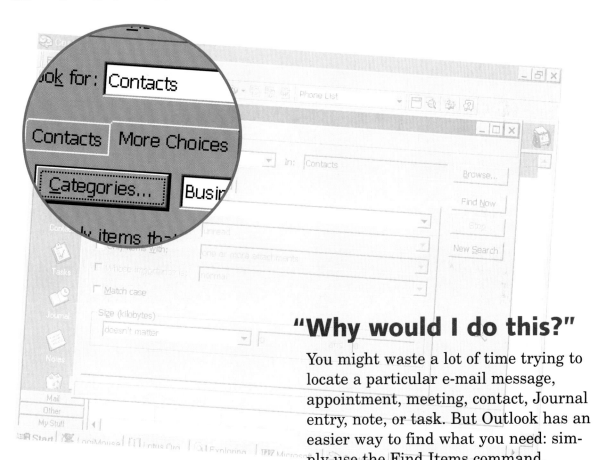

"Why would I do this?"

You might waste a lot of time trying to locate a particular e-mail message, appointment, meeting, contact, Journal entry, note, or task. But Outlook has an easier way to find what you need: simply use the Find Items command.

Once an item is found, you can open it, copy it, move it, delete it, print it—in short, you can do anything you need to do.

Task 64: Searching for a Particular Item

1 Click the **Find Items** button on the Standard toolbar.

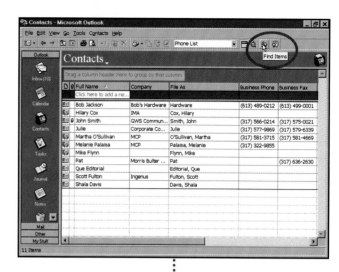

Missing Link

In the Inbox, you can locate all messages related to the current message by using the **Tools, Find All, Related Messages** command. The **Messages From Sender** command on this same menu allows you to locate all messages from the same person as the current message.

2 If you want to search for an item based on its contents, then use the options on the first tab. For example, type MCP in the **Search for the word(s)** text box. To view additional filter options, click the **More Choices** tab.

Puzzled?

The name of the first tab in the Find Items dialog box reflects the name of the Outlook section you're currently in.

3 If you want to locate an item based on its type, use the options on the **More Choices** tab. For example, to search only your business contacts, click **Categories**, select **Business**, then click **OK**. For more filtering choices, click the **Advanced** tab.

Puzzled?

Most likely, you'll only use the options on a single tab within the Filter dialog box to filter your items, although you can combine options as needed.

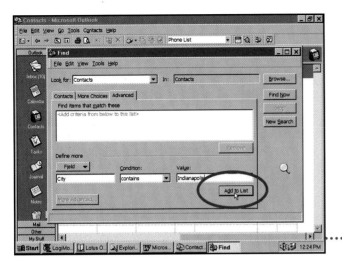

4 To locate items based on the contents of a particular field, use the **Advanced** tab. Select a field from the **Field** list, select a condition (such as equal to) and a value, then click **Add to List.** Repeat to add more fields.

5 When you're through making your selections, click **Find Now**.

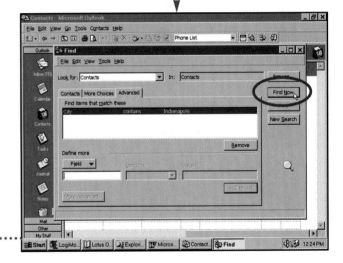

6 The items that match the criteria you selected are displayed at the bottom of the dialog box. To return to Outlook, click the **Close** box. ■

Missing Link

You can copy, move, delete, or print the items displayed in the Find Items list. To open an item, double-click it.

211

PART IX

Using Outlook with Other Office 97 Programs

ONE OF THE NICEST THINGS ABOUT WINDOWS 95 is how it allows programs to work together. With Windows 95, you can easily copy or cut data from one document and then paste it into another. This idea of working together is carried one step further in the Office 97 suite of programs.

With Office 97, you can integrate the data in Outlook with the documents you create. For example, if you want to send out a mass mailing to all of your major clients, you can easily import your Contacts list into Word and then use it to create multiple letters.

On the other hand, you don't have to do something so grand to get the best out of all your Office programs. If you want to create a letter to a particular client, you can import just his address from the Contacts list into Word. You can also use the Contacts list to create memos in Word as well.

In fact, you may already be using Word with Outlook, as your e-mail editor. Although Outlook comes with its own editing program for creating e-mail messages, you may wish to use Word instead, since doing so allows you to take advantage of Word's abilities to spell check words instantly, add tables and graphs, and add emphasis to your words.

You can export data to any of your Office programs, not just Word. For example, you might want to export your Contact list into an Excel spreadsheet, in order to track the amount of time you spend with each client.

You don't have to use your Office data in Outlook, although you may find it convenient. For example, if you want to include some sales figures with an e-mail message, you can start Excel from Outlook, create the sales worksheet, and then, with the click of a mouse, include your worksheet in an e-mail message.

Sometimes you may wish to switch to an Office program and create something that has nothing to do with Outlook. That's OK; Outlook makes it easy to start any new Office file simply by selecting the type of file you want to create from its File, New menu.

In this part, you'll learn how to work with all your Office programs, as needed, whenever you're using Outlook.

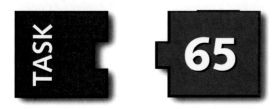

TASK

65

Creating an Office 97 Document from Within Outlook

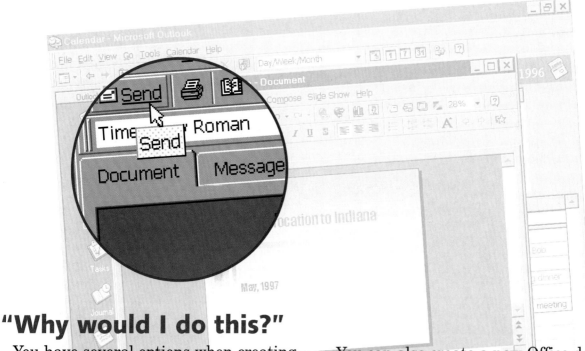

"Why would I do this?"

You have several options when creating an Office document within Outlook. For example, you might want to create a document to include with an e-mail message. Or you might wish to post a new document to an Outlook folder, such as a folder you've created, or a public folder on your company's network.

You can also create a new Office document within Outlook, and save that file to your hard disk. Such a file does not have to be included in any Outlook item—it's as if you created the file through the normal process. Creating files this way is convenient, since Outlook saves you the hassle of having to start the Office program manually.

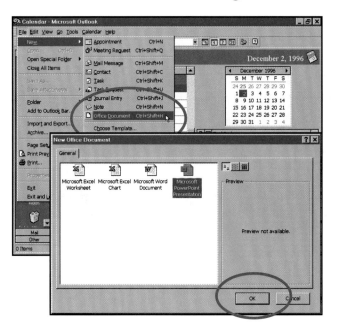

1 To create an Office document for use within Outlook, open the **File** menu, select **New**, then select **Office Document**.

2 Click the icon for the program you want to use, then click OK.

Missing Link

You can also double-click the Office icon you want in order to start its program.

3 Select **Send the document to someone** to include the new file in an e-mail message, or **Post the document in this folder** to save the document in a folder which is accessible to Outlook users, such as a public folder. Click **OK**.

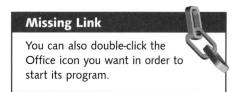

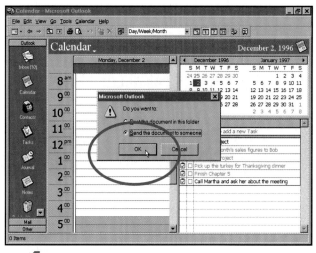

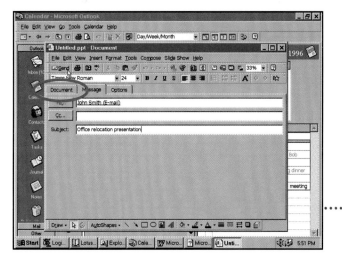

4 If you're creating a file to include with an e-mail message, then enter the necessary data, such as the recipient's address and a Subject. Then click the **Document** tab.

Puzzled?

Even though you're starting the Office program for use within Outlook, all of its tools are still available, such as the drawing tools.

5 Create your new document and click **Send** to send it in an e-mail message.

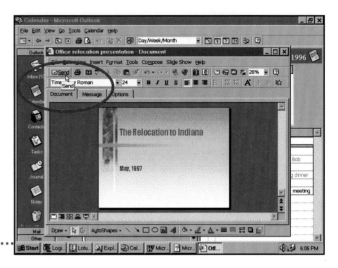

> **Puzzled?**
>
> To view the contents of the document you created later on, you must open the e-mail message and then click the **Documents** tab.

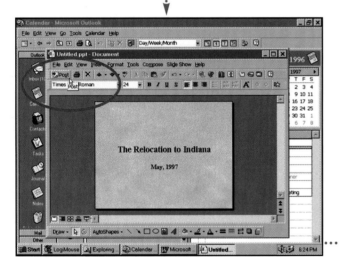

6 If you're saving the new file to a public folder, create the file in the usual manner, then click **Post**.

> **Missing Link**
>
> The file is posted to the current folder.

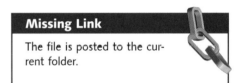

7 If you want to create a new Office document to save to your hard disk, click the **Other** button on the Outlook bar.

> **Missing Link**
>
> Starting a program from within Outlook is similar to opening it from the Start menu.

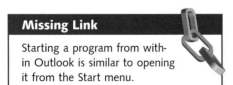

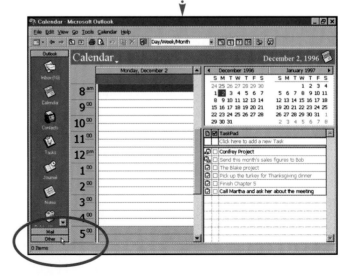

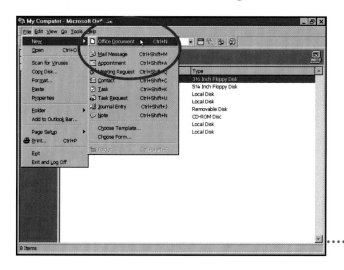

8 Open the **File** menu, select **New**, then select **Office Document**.

9 Click the appropriate tab, then click the icon for the type of file you want to create. Click **OK**.

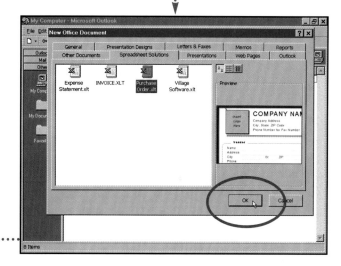

10 Create your document in the usual manner. Save it, then click the program's **Close** button to exit the program and return to Outlook. ■

66

Using Word as Your E-Mail Editor

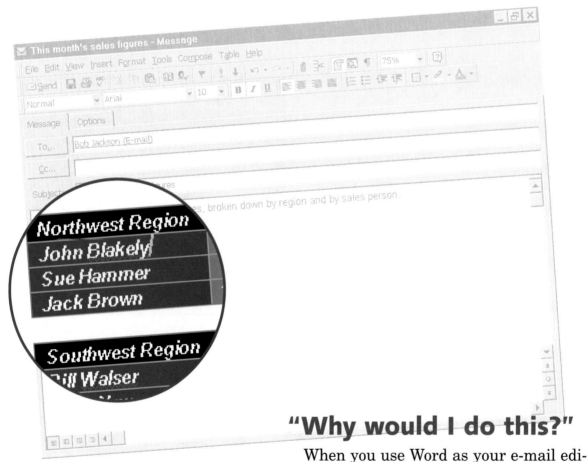

"Why would I do this?"

When you use Word as your e-mail editor, you have full access to all of its features, including instant spell-checking, tables, worksheets, columns, and drawing tools, among others.

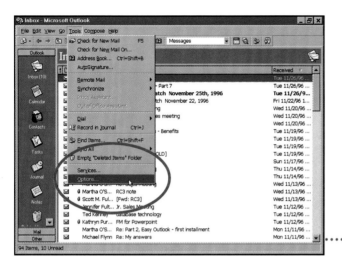

1 Open the **Tools** menu and select **Options**.

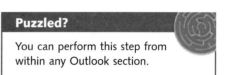

Puzzled?

You can perform this step from within any Outlook section.

2 Click the **E-Mail** tab if needed. Then select the Use **Microsoft Word as the e-mail editor** option. Click **OK**.

Missing Link

A check mark indicates that the option is currently selected.

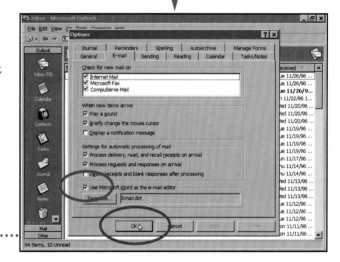

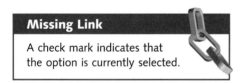

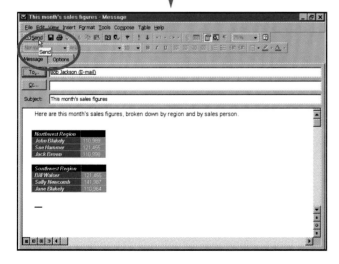

3 When you create a new e-mail message, the menu and toolbars that appear will be Word's. You can use any Word tool you like to create your e-mail message. ■

Missing Link

If you find that using Word takes up too much of your computer's memory (and slows things down) you can return to the regular editor by repeating these steps.

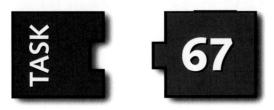

TASK

67

Exporting Data to an Office 97 Program

"Why would I do this?"

You can export any of your Outlook data for use in an Office program. For example, you might want to export your contact list for use within Excel or Word.

When you export data, you can select from several formats, including popular Office program formats such as Microsoft Excel and Microsoft Access.

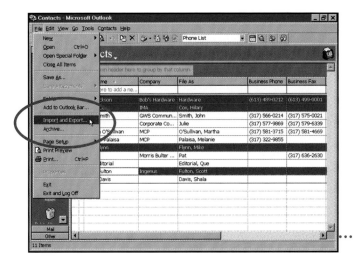

1 Switch to the folder which contains the items you want to export. Open the **File** menu and select **Import and Export**.

Puzzled?

All of the entries in the current folder will be exported. If you want to export only some of the entries, then copy the items you want into a separate folder.

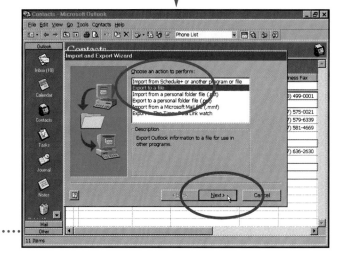

2 Select **Export** to a file and click **Next>**.

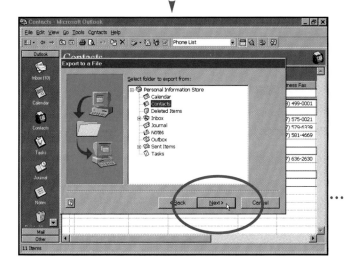

3 Verify that the correct folder is selected, then click **Next>**.

4 Select the program to which you want to export, such as Microsoft Excel. Click **Next>**.

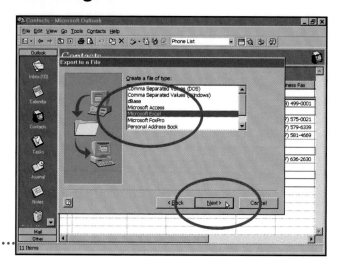

Puzzled?

If you're trying to export data to Word or PowerPoint, or a non-Office program, then select Comma Separated Values or Tab Separated Values.

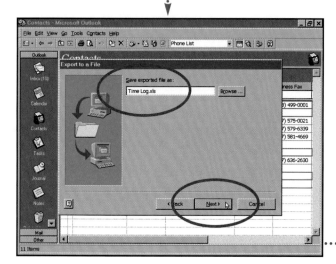

5 Type a name for the exported file, and click **Next>**.

Puzzled?

Files have specific extensions which help the program which use them to identify them as their own. For example, Microsoft Excel uses the extension .XLS to identify its files.

6 Verify that the correct action is listed, then select **Finish**. ■

Missing Link

If you need to export fields other than the standard name, address, and phone number, click Map Custom Headings and select the items you'd like to use. Click **OK** to return to the Import and Export dialog box.

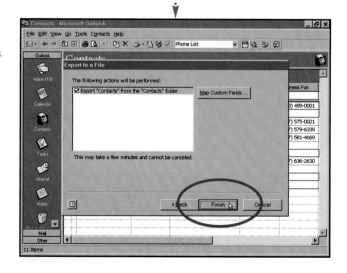

Creating a Mail Merge in Word from the Contact List

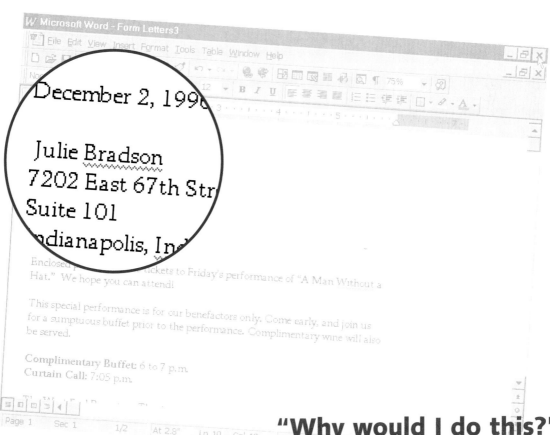

"Why would I do this?"

Using your Contacts list and Word, you can quickly create multiple letters (form letters), mailing labels, or envelopes. Using the power of both Outlook and Word saves you the trouble of creating each letter, label, or envelope manually.

Task 68: Creating a Mail Merge in Word from the Contact List

1 In Word, open the **Tools** menu and select **Mail Merge.**

2 Click **Create**, and select the type of document you want to create: letter, label, or envelope.

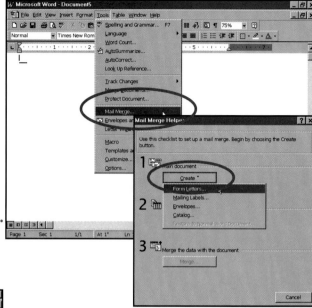

3 If the current window is blank, you can use it to create your merge document by clicking **Active Window**. To create a new document, click **New Main Document**.

4 Click **Get Data** and select **Use Address Book**.

Puzzled?

If you want to export something other than the standard name and address fields, export the Contact list using the **File**, **Import and Export** command, and select the fields you want with the Map Custom Heading button on the Recipient tab. Then, to use the exported file in Word, click Open Data Source.

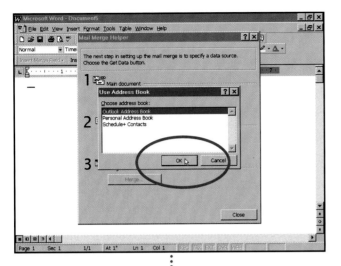

5 Select the **Address** folder you want to use, then click **OK**.

> **Puzzled?**
>
> If the contacts you want to merge are located in a special folder (and it doesn't appear in the list), then switch to Outlook, select the folder you want to add to the Address Book list, open the **File** menu, select **Folder**, and select **Properties**. Click the **Outlook Address Book** tab. Select **Show this folder as an e-mail Address Book**. Enter a name for the address book folder and click **OK**.

6 Click **Edit Main Document**.

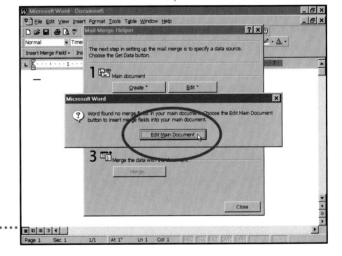

7 If your creating a letter, enter its text. Wherever you want to insert a field from the Contact list, click the **Insert Merge Field** button on the Mail Merge toolbar. Click a field name to insert it at the cursor.

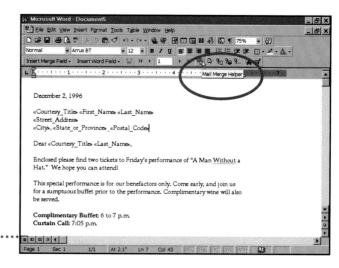

8 When you're done, click **Mail Merge Helper** on the Mail Merge toolbar.

9 To merge selected items from the Contact List, click **Query Options**.

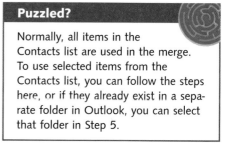

Puzzled?

Normally, all items in the Contacts list are used in the merge. To use selected items from the Contacts list, you can follow the steps here, or if they already exist in a separate folder in Outlook, you can select that folder in Step 5.

10 Select a field and a value to compare to the items in the Contacts list. You can enter more than one value if you like. When you're done, click **OK**.

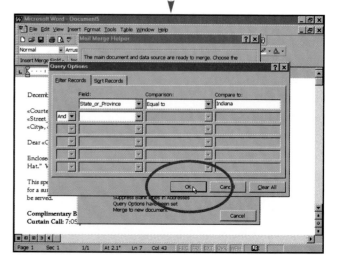

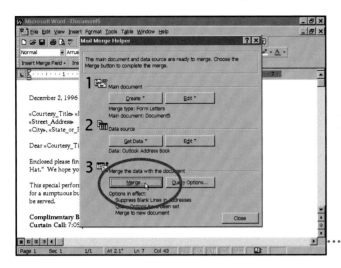

11 Click **Merge**.

12 Select how you want the merged documents to appear: as a document file, an e-mail, a fax, and so on. Then click **Merge**.

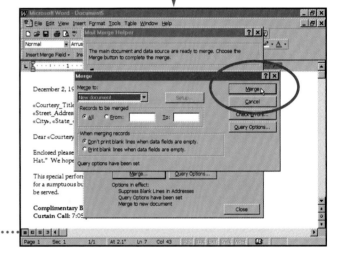

13 The selected contacts are merged with your document. Print or save the document as needed; when you're through, click Word's **Close** button to return to Outlook. ■

Reference

Installing Outlook

A Guide to Outlook's
Toolbars

A Guide to the Icons Used
in Outlook

▲ ● ■ ▲ ● ■ ▲ ●

Installing Outlook

Whether you have Microsoft Office 97 or just Outlook 97, these steps walk you through installing Outlook on your computer's hard disk:

1. Insert Outlook disk 1 in the floppy drive, or if you have an Office CD, insert the CD in the CD-ROM drive. If you use the CD, you won't have to insert any of the disks during installation; you work with the CD only.

2. If you're using the Office CD, then skip to step 3. Otherwise, open the **Start** menu and choose **Run** to display the Run dialog box. In the Command Line text box, type a:\setup (for installation from a floppy) or d:\setup (for installation from a CD) and press **Enter**.

3. Click the **Install Microsoft Office** icon. Read the copyright message and click **Continue**.

4. Enter your **Name** and **Organization** and click **OK**. Click **OK** again to confirm.

5. The Product ID is displayed. Click **OK**.

6. (Optional) You can change the directory to which Outlook is installed, but that's not really necessary. However, you might want to change to a different drive if the current drive does not have enough available disk space.

7. When prompted, select the **Typical installation**. This installs all of the essential features.

8. Select the options you'd like installed, and click **Continue**.

9. If Setup finds a previous version of Microsoft Office, click **Yes** to remove it.

10. You'll see a message when the installation is complete. Click **OK**. (If you have a modem, you can click Online Registration instead, to register your copy of Outlook.

Updating Outlook

If you have a connection to the Internet, Microsoft provides an easy way for you to update your Outlook program with the latest enhancements.

Right now, those enhancements include the Rules Wizard, a tool that enables you to set up rules for processing incoming e-mail; the 3-pane at the bottom of the Inbox window, without actually opening it; vCards support, for creating a new contact using an electronic business card found on the Internet; support for America Online; additional filters for importing address books from other programs; Crystal Reports, a program that enables you to create custom reports with Outlook; and support for Times Data Link Watch. Of course, there are more items being added every week, so it's worth checking it out.

To update your Outlook program, connect to the Internet, then open the Help menu, select Microsoft on the Web, and then select Free Stuff. Your Web browser will start and find a page with the latest Outlook inhancements. Click a link to download whichever enhancements you want. Then log off the Internet.

To install an enhancement, exit Outlook. Then open Explorer and double-click the enhancement file. The installation happens automatically. When it's through, click OK, and you're done.

A Guide to Outlook's Toolbars

Underneath Outlook's menu bar is the Standard toolbar. On this toolbar are buttons, which, when clicked, allow you to perform some common tasks such as creating a new mail message.

As you move from section to section in Outlook, the buttons on the Standard toolbar change, in order to provide access to the common tasks of that section. For example, when you're in Calendar, you'll see buttons for displaying a day, a week, or a month's worth of appointments. Switch to the Inbox, and these buttons are replaced with ones that allow you to reply and forward your messages.

Use this guide to identify the purpose of each toolbar button.

The Inbox, Sent Items, and Outbox Toolbar

Button	Description
	Create new message
	Move back to the previously viewed Outlook section

The Inbox, Sent Items, and Outbox Toolbar (continued)

Button	Description
	Move forward to the next previously viewed Outlook section
	Move up one level within Outlook's folders
	Display the Folder List
	Print messages
	Preview before you print
	Undo last action
	Move an item to another folder
	Delete an item
	Reply to a message
	Reply to all recipient's of an original message
	Forward a message
	Display the Address Book
Messages ▾	Change the view
	Group items by a particular column
	Display the first few lines of unread messages

Button	Description
	Locate a message
	Display the Office Assistant

The Calendar Toolbar

Button	Description
	Create a new appointment
	Plan a meeting
	Display today's appointments
	Display a day's worth of appointments
	Display a week's worth of appointments
	Display a month's worth of appointments

The Contacts Toolbar

Button	Description
	Create a new contact
	Dial a contact
	Send a message to a contact
	Create a meeting with a contact

The Contacts Toolbar (continued)

Button	Description
	Visit a contact's Web page
	Display notes on a contact

The Tasks Toolbar

Button	Description
	Create a new task
	Display notes on a task

The Journal Toolbar

Button	Description
	Create a new Journal entry
	Display today's entries
	Display a day's worth of entries
	Display a week's worth of entries
	Display a month's worth of entries

The Notes Toolbar

Button	Description
	Create a new note
	Display notes as large icons
	Display notes as small icons

The Deleted Items Toolbar

Button	Description
	Create a new message
	Reply to a message
Messages	Reply to all recipient's of an original message
	Forward a message
	Display the Address Book
	Display the first few lines of a message

The My Computer Toolbar

Button	Description
	Create a new Office document
	Display the contents of a network drive

The My Computer Toolbar (continued)

Button	Description
	Disconnect from a network drive
	Display any notes attached to an item

The Remote Toolbar

Button	Description
	Connect to a remote mail server
	Disconnect from a remote mail server
	Mark a message for retrieval
	Mark to receive a copy of a message
	Delete a message without retrieving it
	Unmark a marked message
	Unmark all marked messages
Close	Remove the Remote toolbar

A Guide to the Icons Used in Outlook

Outlook uses many icons (small pictures) in its listings to provide additional information about an item. For example, if an e-mail message has been marked important, it will appear with a small exclamation mark. In this section, you'll learn what the various icons used in Outlook are for.

Icons Used in the Inbox

Button	Description
	Message is of high importance
	Message is of low importance
	Read message
	Unread message
	Forwarded message
	Replied to message
	Saved or Unsent message
	Protected message
	Message with a digital signature
	Microsoft Mail form
	Posted message
	An attempt has been made to recall this message
	Message was successfully recalled
	Message was unsuccessfully recalled
	Message was successfully delivered

Icons Used in the Inbox (continued)

Button	Description
	Message has been read
	Message was not delivered successfully
	Message was not read
	Accepted meeting request
	Tentatively accepted meeting request
	Declined meeting request
	Cancelled meeting
	Task request
	Accepted task
	Declined task
	Folder is offline; message is unavailable
	Message has an attachment
	Message is flagged for follow up
	Message is flagged as complete
	A Remote message exists on the mail server, but has yet been downloaded to your system

Button	Description
	A Remote message is marked for download
	A Remote message is marked for copy and download

Icons Used in the Calendar

Icon	Description
	Appointment
	Click this icon to see calendar items that do not fit in the current view
	Meeting
	Meeting request
	Recurring appointment
	Recurring meeting
	Recurring meeting or appointment
	Reminder for the appointment or meeting
	Private meeting or appointment
	Start time of the appointment or meeting
	End time of the appointment or meeting

Icons Used in the Calendar (continued)

Icon	Description
	Calendar item has an attachment
	Folder is offline; calendar item is unavailable

Icons Used in the Contacts List

Icon	Description
	Activities for this contact are being automatically recorded in Journal
	Contact
	Contact has an attachment
	Folder is offline; contact is unavailable

Icons Used in the Tasks List

Icon	Description
	Accepted task
	Completed task
	Declined task
	High importance task
	Low importance task
	Recurring task

Icon	Description
	Task
	This task has been assigned to another person
	This task has been assigned to you
	This task has an attachment
	Uncompleted task
	Folder is offline; task is unavailable

Icons Used in the Journal

Icon	Description
	Appointment
	Appointment request, appointment response, meeting, meeting request, meeting response
	Conversation
	Document
	E-mail message
	Fax
	Letter
	Microsoft Access database

Icons Used in the Journal (continued)

Icon	Description
	Microsoft Excel workbook
	Microsoft Office Binder document
	Microsoft PowerPoint presentation
	Microsoft Word document
	Note
	Phone call
	Task
	Task request, task response
	Journal item has an attachment
	Folder is offline; journal entry is unavailable

Index

Symbols

Index

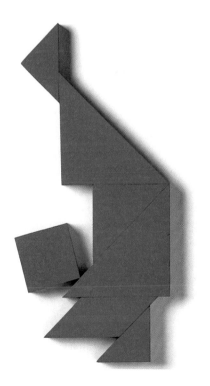

Complete and Return this Card
for a *FREE* Computer Book Catalog

Thank you for purchasing this book! You have purchased a superior computer book written expressly for your needs. To continue to provide the kind of up-to-date, pertinent coverage you've come to expect from us, we need to hear from you. Please take a minute to complete and return this self-addressed, postage-paid form. In return, we'll send you a free catalog of all our computer books on topics ranging from word processing to programming and the internet.

Mr. ☐   Mrs. ☐   Ms. ☐   Dr. ☐

Name (first) ☐☐☐☐☐☐☐☐☐☐☐ (M.I.) ☐   (last) ☐☐☐☐☐☐☐☐☐☐☐☐☐☐☐

Address ☐☐☐☐☐☐☐☐☐☐☐☐☐☐☐☐☐☐☐☐☐☐☐☐☐☐☐☐

☐☐☐☐☐☐☐☐☐☐☐☐☐☐☐☐☐☐☐☐☐☐☐☐☐☐☐☐

City ☐☐☐☐☐☐☐☐☐☐☐☐☐☐☐☐   State ☐☐   Zip ☐☐☐☐☐ ☐☐☐☐

Phone ☐☐☐ ☐☐☐ ☐☐☐☐   Fax ☐☐☐ ☐☐☐ ☐☐☐☐

Company Name ☐☐☐☐☐☐☐☐☐☐☐☐☐☐☐☐☐☐☐☐☐☐☐☐☐☐☐☐

E-mail address ☐☐☐☐☐☐☐☐☐☐☐☐☐☐☐☐☐☐☐☐☐☐☐☐☐☐☐☐

1. Please check at least (3) influencing factors for purchasing this book.

Front or back cover information on book ☐
Special approach to the content ☐
Completeness of content ☐
Author's reputation ☐
Publisher's reputation ☐
Book cover design or layout ☐
Index or table of contents of book ☐
Price of book ☐
Special effects, graphics, illustrations ☐
Other (Please specify): _____ ☐

2. How did you first learn about this book?

Saw in Macmillan Computer Publishing catalog ☐
Recommended by store personnel ☐
Saw the book on bookshelf at store ☐
Recommended by a friend ☐
Received advertisement in the mail ☐
Saw an advertisement in: _____ ☐
Read book review in: _____ ☐
Other (Please specify): _____ ☐

3. How many computer books have you purchased in the last six months?

This book only ☐   3 to 5 books ☐
2 books ☐   More than 5 ☐

4. Where did you purchase this book?

Bookstore ☐
Computer Store ☐
Consumer Electronics Store ☐
Department Store ☐
Office Club ☐
Warehouse Club ☐
Mail Order ☐
Direct from Publisher ☐
Internet site ☐
Other (Please specify): _____ ☐

5. How long have you been using a computer?

☐ Less than 6 months   ☐ 6 months to a year
☐ 1 to 3 years   ☐ More than 3 years

6. What is your level of experience with personal computers and with the subject of this book?

	With PCs	With subject of book
New	☐	☐
Casual	☐	☐
Accomplished	☐	☐
Expert	☐	☐

Source Code ISBN: 0-7897-1141-9

7. Which of the following best describes your job title?

Administrative Assistant .... ☐
Coordinator .... ☐
Manager/Supervisor .... ☐
Director .... ☐
Vice President .... ☐
President/CEO/COO .... ☐
Lawyer/Doctor/Medical Professional .... ☐
Teacher/Educator/Trainer .... ☐
Engineer/Technician .... ☐
Consultant .... ☐
Not employed/Student/Retired .... ☐
Other (Please specify): _____ ☐

8. Which of the following best describes the area of the company your job title falls under?

Accounting .... ☐
Engineering .... ☐
Manufacturing .... ☐
Operations .... ☐
Marketing .... ☐
Sales .... ☐
Other (Please specify): _____ ☐

Comments: _____
_____
_____

9. What is your age?

Under 20 .... ☐
21-29 .... ☐
30-39 .... ☐
40-49 .... ☐
50-59 .... ☐
60-over .... ☐

10. Are you:

Male .... ☐
Female .... ☐

11. Which computer publications do you read regularly? (Please list)

_____
_____
_____
_____
_____
_____
_____
_____
_____
_____

Fold here and scotch-tape to mail.

Check out Que® Books on the World Wide Web
http://www.quecorp.com

As the biggest software release in computer history, Windows 95 continues to redefine the computer industry. Click here for the latest info on our Windows 95 books

Examine the latest releases in word processing, spreadsheets, operating systems, and suites

Find out about new additions to our site, new bestsellers and hot topics

Make computing quick and easy with these products designed exclusively for new and casual users

The Internet, The World Wide Web, CompuServe®, America Online®, Prodigy® —it's a world of ever-changing information. Don't get left behind!

In-depth information on high-end topics: find the best reference books for databases, programming, networking, and client/server technologies

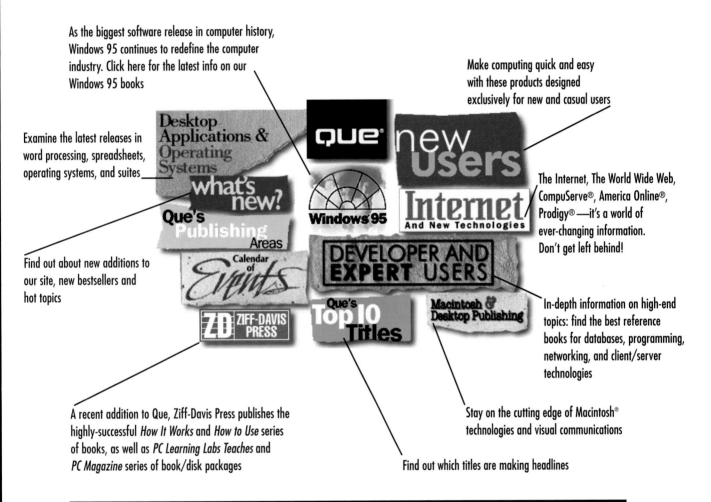

A recent addition to Que, Ziff-Davis Press publishes the highly-successful *How It Works* and *How to Use* series of books, as well as *PC Learning Labs Teaches* and *PC Magazine* series of book/disk packages

Find out which titles are making headlines

Stay on the cutting edge of Macintosh® technologies and visual communications

With 6 separate publishing groups, Que develops products for many specific market segments and areas of computer technology. Explore our Web Site and you'll find information on best-selling titles, newly published titles, upcoming products, authors, and much more.

- Stay informed on the latest industry trends and products available
- Visit our online bookstore for the latest information and editions
- Download software from Que's library of the best shareware and freeware

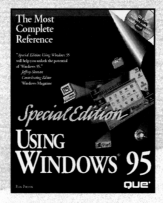
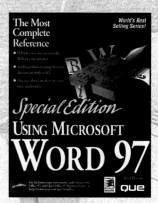

MACMILLAN COMPUTER PUBLISHING USA

A VIACOM COMPANY

Technical -----Support:

If you need assistance with the information in this book or with a CD/Disk accompanying the book, please access the Knowledge Base on our Web site at **http://www.superlibrary.com/general/support**. Our most Frequently Asked Questions are answered there. If you do not find the answer to your questions on our Web site, you may contact Macmillan Technical Support **(317) 581-3833** or e-mail us at **support@mcp.com**.